Pathfinder®Guides

GW00676527

Kent

Walks

Fully revised by
David Hancock

Contents

At-a-glance

Walk		Page	![route]	![start] 🏁	![distance] ⛰	![ascent]	![time] 🕐
1	**Cobham**	8	Cobham	TQ 671 685	3½ miles (5.6km)	215ft (65m)	1½ hrs
2	**Elham and Acrise**	10	Elham	TR 177 438	4 miles (6.5km)	410ft (125m)	2 hrs
3	**Stodmarsh and the Stour Valley**	12	Stodmarsh Nature Reserve	TR 221 609	4¼ miles (6.8km)	n/a	2 hrs
4	**Brookland and Fairfield**	14	Brookland	TQ 988 257	5 miles (8km)	n/a	2 hrs
5	**Appledore and the Royal Military Canal**	16	Appledore	TQ 955 296	5¼ miles (8.4km)	180ft (55m)	2½ hrs
6	**Sutton Valence and Ulcombe**	18	Sutton Valence	TQ 814 492	5¼ miles (8.4km)	395ft (120m)	2½ hrs
7	**Westerham and Chartwell**	21	Westerham church	TQ 447 540	5¼ miles (8.4km)	705ft (215m)	2½ hrs
8	**Sandwich and Sandwich Bay**	24	Sandwich	TR 332 582	6 miles (9.6km)	n/a	2½ hrs
9	**Farthing Common, Postling and Tolsford Hill**	28	Farthing Common	TR 136 403	5½ miles (8km)	820ft (250m)	3 hrs
10	**Lamberhurst and Hook Green**	30	Lamberhurst	TQ 676 362	6 miles (9.6km)	720ft (220m)	3 hrs
11	**Knole Park, Godden Green and One Tree Hill**	33	One Tree Hill, near Sevenoaks	TQ 558 531	6 miles (9.5km)	705ft (215m)	3 hrs
12	**Mereworth Woods and West Peckham**	36	Mereworth church	TQ 660 537	6¼ miles (10km)	655ft (200m)	3 hrs
13	**Egerton and Pluckley**	39	Egerton	TQ 906 473	6¾ miles (10.8km)	360ft (110m)	3 hrs
14	**Ightham Mote and Oldbury Hill**	42	Ightham Mote	TQ 584 536	6¾ miles (10.8km)	900ft (275m)	3½ hrs
15	**Benenden and Rolvenden**	45	Benenden	TQ 810 328	7 miles (11.2km)	590ft (180m)	3½ hrs
16	**Shoreham and Lullingstone Park**	48	Shoreham	TQ 518 615	7 miles (11.2km)	690ft (210m)	3½ hrs
17	**Ancient and modern woodland around Blean**	51	Gypsy Corner	TR 136 629	7¼ miles (11.6km)	295ft (90m)	3½ hrs
18	**Cranbrook and Sissinghurst**	54	Cranbrook church	TQ 776 362	7¼ miles (11.6km)	410ft (125m)	3½ hrs
19	**Penshurst and Chiddingstone**	57	Penshurst	TQ 526 437	7½ miles (12km)	410ft (125m)	3½ hrs
20	**Linton and Boughton Monchelsea**	60	Linton church	TQ 754 502	7½ miles (12km)	625ft (190m)	3½ hrs
21	**Reculver and the Wantsum Walk**	63	Reculver	TR 226 693	8¼ miles (13.2km)	n/a	3½ hrs
22	**The Isle of Harty**	66	Leysdown-on-Sea	TR 044 697	8 miles (12.8km)	100ft (30m)	3½ hrs
23	**Hollingbourne and Thurnham**	70	Hollingbourne	TQ 844 553	7½ miles (12km)	1,115ft (340m)	4 hrs
24	**St Margaret's Bay and The South Foreland**	73	St Margaret's at Cliffe	TR 358 447	8¼ miles (13.2km)	1,065ft (325m)	4 hrs
25	**Wye and Crundale Downs**	76	Wye church	TR 054 468	8½ miles (13.5km)	1,050ft (320m)	4 hrs
26	**Bridge, Bishopsbourne and Pett Bottom**	80	Bridge	TR 183 541	9½ miles (15.2km)	805ft (245m)	4½ hrs
27	**Oare Marshes, the Swale and Luddenham**	84	Oare	TR 007 628	10 miles (16km)	165ft (50m)	4½ hrs
28	**Chilham, Godmersham and the Stour Valley**	88	The Square, Chilham	TR 068 535	10¼ miles (16.4km)	1,065ft (325m)	5 hrs

Comments

A short walk along peaceful downland paths from Cobham village, noted for its fine church and associations with Charles Dickens, to Henley Down, where you have glorious views across Luddesdown nestling in a valley.

From the ancient settlement of Elham this route strikes out to Acrise, a forgotten village with a tiny, hidden church. There are fine views from many of the field paths.

Birdwatchers should bring binoculars on this level walk through the diverse wetland habitat of Stodmarsh Nature Reserve in the Stour Valley. Hides offer the perfect vantage point to observe the rich bird life.

Two fascinating Romney Marsh churches are the focus of this atmospheric low-level walk through sheep-filled pastures and open arable fields and along quiet lanes from historic Brookland village.

The canal was dug in 1804 as an aid to defence at a time when invasion by Napoleon was feared, and restored as a defence work in 1940. Today it makes for a fine walking route.

The ruined 12th-century castle at Sutton Valence begins this walk, through attractive countryside and using part of the Greensand Way with far-reaching Wealden views on the return route.

Chartwell, seen on this glorious woodland walk, was the country home of Sir Winston Churchill. An imposing statue of the former prime minister can be seen on the green in Westerham.

Pretty Sandwich was once a centre for smugglers, but these days you are more likely to encounter golfers; the route crosses famous Royal St George's Golf Course on the return from Sandwich Bay.

A short, highly enjoyable route across downland. Lofty grassy paths thread through steep-sided valleys and along the crest of the North Downs, the latter affording splendid Wealden views.

One of the most beautiful views in any of the walks is featured in this route, which explores the landscape around Lamberhurst by way of field and woodland paths.

The walk begins at One Tree Hill, a superb viewpoint, and passes the largest house in Britain, Knole. The ancient Knole Park, through which half this walk passes, is home to a herd of deer.

West Peckham has the classic look of an English village. It forms the centrepiece to this invigorating walk, through woodland on the outward leg and along the top of the Wealden ridge on the return.

Orchard, field and farmland paths lead to Pluckley, made famous in the TV series *The Darling Buds of May*, returning to Egerton along the Greensand Way, with glorious views across the Weald and the North Downs.

The remarkable 13th-century house of Ightham Mote (complete with moat, as its name suggests) begins a fine woodland walk with some magnificent views from the hills along the way.

Following the High Weald Landscape Trail, this peaceful rural ramble explores gently rolling countryside between the classic Wealden villages of Benenden and Rolvenden.

A very pleasant route through the beautiful Darent Valley that passes Lullingstone Castle, which has a fascinating World Garden and lies near to the site of a Roman villa.

There are few long views on this route, making it ideal for a misty autumn day. Attractions along the way include beautiful woodlands and the course of the world's first steam passenger railway.

This route proceeds through fields and bluebell woods to Sissinghurst, where the remains of a Tudor mansion lie in the National Trust property of Sissinghurst Garden.

Churches, a mansion and a castle are features on this walk, which explores the Eden Valley to the timeless National Trust village of Chiddingstone, returning through the glorious Penshurst Estate.

Beginning with views down over the Weald, this walk proceeds into parkland and takes in the fine house of Boughton Monchelsea, set in the midst of a deer park. A shorter version is possible.

Reculver was a Roman settlement, and some traces remain of their buildings, along with the ruins of a 1st-century monastery. The walk follows the sea wall and returns over lonely marshes.

The landscape around Harty is paradise for birdwatchers, with wide expanses and huge sky. There is a shorter version, but walkers who shun the short cut will be rewarded with a pub at the farthest point.

Walkers have the chance to see some fine views from the top of the ridge along this route. The path has many ups and downs, making this a physically challenging route.

An enjoyable route leading down to St Margaret's Bay and the White Cliffs Trail leading to South Foreland Lighthouse, with an optional cliff top walk to Langdon Cliff Visitor Centre for views across Dover Harbour.

Some beautiful views can be savoured on this fine downland route, on both the North Downs Way along the crest of the downs, and over the splendid, isolated Crundale Down.

This route rambles through the landscape around Canterbury, passing through orchards, parkland and woodland and taking in two attractive villages.

The desolate marsh landscape around the Swale may not be to everyone's taste, but some will love the isolation of this walk, especially birdwatchers as the walk passes through Oare Marsh Nature Reserve.

Medieval Chilham is steeped in history, reflected in the layout of this showpiece village. The return includes a stretch alongside the Stour and on a lakeside, with good opportunities for birdwatching.

Introduction to Kent

Kent's earliest visitors entered the county via the land bridge which until about 6,000 years ago joined England to the Continent. Kent is a maritime county, and even after the land bridge had been severed it remained the easiest landfall for travellers from Europe. Julius Caesar landed at Deal believing that the inhabitants of Kent would be the most civilised in Britain, since it was the closest point to Gaul, and a century later Emperor Claudius arrived to colonise Britain and used the wide channels around the Isle of Thanet as the principal anchorage for his fleet. A thriving town, complete with triumphal arch and amphitheatre, grew up around his castle at Richborough. To create an infrastructure of communications, Claudius built Watling Street between Dover and London, a straight road below the north edge of the North Downs, the route of which is followed by the A2.

In those days the landscape of the county was hardly touched by man. This began to change in the late Middle Ages when the invention of gunpowder transformed weapons of war. Great oaks of the Weald were cut down to make charcoal for the smelting of iron, which

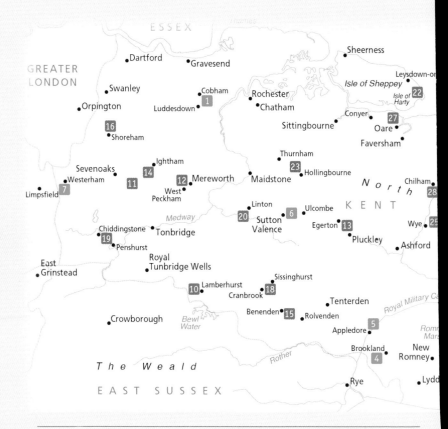

was cast to make cannons for warships built on the Thames and the Medway (using more Kentish oak). Up to 2,000 trees would be felled to make one man-of-war.

In the 14th century Edward III encouraged Flemish weavers to come to England, believing their skills would improve the quality cloth industry. Many settled in Kent, and the wool trade grew rapidly. Immigrants from the Low Countries also introduced hops as an ingredient of beer, though many Englishmen preferred the traditional flavour of cinnamon and cloves for some time. Eventually the brewing industry was won over to hops, and Kent was

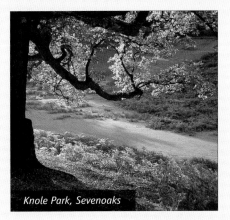
Knole Park, Sevenoaks

soon the main centre for growing them. However, the oast houses used for drying hops only appeared in the 18th and 19th centuries.

More Huguenots arrived in the 16th–17th centuries and drained the flat land between Sandwich and Canterbury to grow fruit and vegetables. The success of their work gave Kent the name 'Garden of England'.

Sheep continued to graze the down-lands until the 20th century, and over the centuries the grass was closely cropped to become the springy turf which made walking such a pleasure. Fortunately a little of this survives on preserved parts of the downs such as at Wye (*Walk 25*) but most of Kent's landscape has been transformed by the agricultural revolution. Open downland has been replaced with vast unhedged fields of wheat, rape-seed or flax, and prairie-like fields have been made from grazing marshes which were formerly feeding grounds for migrant as well as native birds.

However, walkers in Kent enjoy a number of benefits, primarily long-distance footpaths. The most celebrated of these is the 141-mile (226km) North

Downs Way. This route, combined with the Pilgrims' Way, can be extended westwards all the way to Winchester. The Greensand Way follows another geological feature: the outcrop of greensand south of the downs. The route begins at Leith Hill in Surrey and ends at Ham Street, just south of Ashford, a distance of 100 miles (160km). A third route is the Wealdway. This 80-mile (128km) footpath runs from Eastbourne to Gravesend, traversing the Weald. Finally there is the Saxon Shore Way, which follows the coastline for 140 miles (225km) from Gravesend to Rye. These paths are kept in good order by Kent County Council and our routes make use of parts of all of them. The council welcomes comments on the state of paths (see page 94 for the address).

For the most part strangers to Kent will be delighted at its rare beauty and the variety of its landscape. Vast panoramas can be enjoyed from the crest of the downs. Walks go through ancient woodland and along shoreline paths once frequented by smugglers. The cliffs about Dover and Folkestone evoke a special flavour of history and romance while the marshes of Romney Marsh and the Swale have a wild and lonely beauty. Cottages, farmhouses, medieval churches, and oast houses make the landscape unique to this part of England. It is a wonder that such a countryside survives so close to the capital city. It is hoped that these walks will enable more people to explore and enjoy it.

Practicalities

Unless you are particularly fortunate with the weather it will be best to wear walking boots for nearly all these walks. Wellingtons are only satisfactory for comparatively short routes, although they have advantages in winter when some paths, shared with horses, may be deep in mud.

Many of the routes go into countryside which is truly remote, and if the weather changes there is little in the way of shelter on the crest of the downs or on Swaleside marshland. Unless you have absolute faith in the accuracy of a weather forecast, take warm and waterproof clothing. This is especially important in winter since Kent is known for its heavy snowfall, low temperatures and bitter winds.

Note that a few of the walks do not pass any places offering refreshment. Where refreshments are available be aware of seasonal and evening only opening.

This book includes a list of waypoints alongside the description of the walk, so that you can enjoy the full benefits of gps should you wish to. For more information on using your gps, read the Pathfinder® Guide *GPS for Walkers*, by gps teacher and navigation trainer, Clive Thomas (ISBN 978-0-7117-4445-5). For essential information on map reading and basic navigation, read the Pathfinder® Guide *Map Reading Skills* by outdoor writer, Terry Marsh (ISBN 978-0-7117-4978-8). Both titles are available in bookshops or can be ordered online at www.crimsonpublishing.co.uk

Along the River Great Stour

walk 1

Cobham

Start
Cobham

Distance
3½ miles (5.6km)

Height gain
215 feet (65m)

Approximate time
1½ hours

Route terrain
Field, woodland and orchard paths

Parking
Car park behind the village school

OS maps
Landranger 177 (East London), Explorer 148 (Maidstone & the Medway Towns)

GPS waypoints
 TQ 671 685
Ⓐ TQ 666 671
Ⓑ TQ 658 670

The walk sets out past Cobham's impressive 13th-century church and takes you across downland fields to the hamlet of Henley Street. A gentle climb to the top of Henley Down is rewarded with peaceful views across Luddesdown, where Luddesdown Court is believed to be one of the oldest, continuously occupied houses in Britain. Paths through fields and orchards lead back to Cobham, where the Leather Bottle pub, made famous by Charles Dickens in The Pickwick Papers, *makes a good post-walk refreshment stop.*

Cobham Allow time to linger in pretty Cobham, with its fine collection of historic buildings and associations with Charles Dickens, who lived at Gad's Hill, just over 3 miles away. The 13th-century Church of St Mary Magdalene has an outstanding collection of medieval brasses, the fine buildings of Cobham New College behind the church were endowed as a college for a priest in the 14th century, and the famous, half-timbered Leather Bottle pub features in The Pickwick Papers and is full of Dickens memorabilia. Owletts, a large redbrick 17th-century manor, stands on the outskirts of the village and is owned by the National Trust.

 Turn right along the village street, passing the Village Stores and the **Darnley Arms**. Just before the **Leather Bottle** pub take the tarmac path on the left to the church, signposted Gold Street and Luddesdown. Pass to the right of the church and the buildings of Cobham New College, the rough tarmac path leading to a new extension to the churchyard.

Keep to the main path, go through a small metal gate and keep to the right-hand edge of a large field, passing beneath two sets of power lines to reach the road in the field corner. Turn left across the railway bridge, then just before Batts Cottage take the waymarked path through a gate on the right. Bear left with the paddock fencing and go through a gate in the field corner. Pass between bushes to a stile and cross a small paddock to a kissing-gate. Bear half-right downhill across a field, joining an enclosed path leading to the road in Henley Street Ⓐ.

Turn left for a few paces, cross the stile on the right and walk uphill through a paddock to a stile. Climb the stile and go through the gate beyond and continue to the top of Henley Down on a defined field path. Pass through the kissing-gate on the field boundary and drop down through a thicket to a junction of paths at the top edge of a field. Pause on the conveniently placed bench and savour the view across the peaceful downland valley to Luddesdown Court and church.

Luddesdown Court   Grade I-listed

Luddesdown Court (not open), which stands beside St Peter and Paul Church with its Norman tower, dates from 1100 and has features from Saxon, Norman, Tudor and Jacobean periods. It is considered to be England's oldest continually occupied house.

To visit Luddesdown church, follow the path ahead down into the valley bottom and cross the road to the church, then retrace your steps back up through the field to the bench. Otherwise, turn right along the top edge of the field, the path soon entering a second field and heading towards a pylon. At a waymarker post indicating that you are now on the Wealdway (WW), bear right up steps to a kissing-gate. Enter a field and keep ahead, following the left-hand field edge gently uphill beside woodland to a further gate.

Walk through the wood, enter a field with a pylon and keep right, following the field edge and pass beneath power lines to join a track in the field corner. Follow this beside Henley Wood and remain on the track to pass to the right of a house. The track improves, passing a pond on your right, then where the hedge ends on the left take the arrowed path right into a large field **B**.

At the immediate fork of paths, take the defined path straight ahead, passing to the right of a pylon, and make for the footbridge over the railway on the far side. Enter an orchard and continue ahead, bearing slightly right along a narrow path that meanders through two orchards to reach a road. Cross into the orchard opposite and follow the path through the trees to a line of poplars on the orchard edge.

Follow the path along the orchard edge, looking out for the waymarker that indicates where the route cuts across the top corner of a former orchard, soon to resume its obvious curving path through orchards towards Cobham church, passing close to more pylons, to reach a metal gate accessing the churchyard extension. Retrace your steps back to the car park. ●

SCALE 1:25000 or 2½ INCHES to 1 MILE 4CM to 1KM

Elham and Acrise

Start

Elham

Distance

4 miles (6.5km)

Height gain

410 feet (125m)

Approximate time

2 hours

Route terrain

Field paths, quiet country lanes

P Parking

The Square, Elham

OS maps

Landranger 179 (Canterbury & East Kent) and 189 (Ashford & Romney Marsh), Explorer 138 (Dover, Folkestone & Hythe)

GPS waypoints

TR 177 438
Ⓐ TR 181 436
Ⓑ TR 188 429
Ⓒ TR 198 427
Ⓓ TR 188 439

Ancient Elham lies snug in its valley, clustered about the medieval church, and its attractive situation is well seen at the beginning of this walk from the path which climbs up the steep side of the valley. Field paths lead to Acrise, a forgotten village with a tiny, hidden church. The return is also mainly on field paths which are usually kept clear by farmers where they cross cultivated land.

Walk down Duck Street on the north side of Elham church, ignoring the footpath which crosses the lane on the edge of the village. Climb up the narrow lane and when it bends sharply to the left Ⓐ turn on to the footpath on the right and climb to the field gate and stile. Cross the meadow beyond diagonally up to a stile at the top corner. There are fine views of Elham and its valley from here. After the stile walk across the neck of another field to a fence and then follow this to a gate at the top of the field. The path continues along the field edge on a generous headland and soon reaches a road.

Cross the road on to another pleasant field-edge path which drops down to Standardhill Plantation and a gate, where there is a pond with a pylon standing in it. Climb up by the side of a line of oaks and Scots pines to a gate and a large field at the top Ⓑ. Continue straight across this and down to a gate at the right-hand edge of woodland and by a sign advising that troops exercise on this army training ground using blank amunition. Head for the transformer at the top of the field, make for the stile to the right of it and turn left on to the road.

The second driveway on the right goes to the tiny Acrise church, but the route continues along the road opposite, which goes to Swingfield and Denton. Turn left off this road at a right-hand bend Ⓒ and walk down the drive to the Old Rectory (do not take the bridleway to the left of the drive). Opposite the house climb over a stile on the right, continue to the gate at the corner of the paddock and then walk across the field to a gate on the far side by Parsonage Wood. After another gate on the other side of this copse turn left and head along the edge of the field towards Standardhill Farm.

The path descends to the bottom of a valley, on the other side of which there is a concrete track. Climb up this until it swings to the left. Keep right of the gates along the field edge to a stile and continue through the next field to a gate into the farmyard and thus reach the road.

Turn left and then right down the lane which is opposite the farmhouse. When this bends to the left after a copse

Elham

SCALE 1:25000 or 2½ INCHES to 1 MILE 4CM to 1KM

D take the footpath on the right. Go straight across the field to a boundary corner where another footpath joins from the right. From this point the course of the footpath is obviously half left across the field to its lowest point. Elham again comes into view. Go through a gate and follow the fence down in a south-westerly direction until you reach another gate. After this the path goes straight across a field to a fence. Turn left to a gate and a bridge over the Nail Bourne.

Cross the bridge and then walk diagonally across a meadow to Cock Lane which leads directly into The Square and the **Kings Arms** pub. ●

Start
Stodmarsh

Distance
4¼ miles (6.8km)

Height gain
Negligible

Approximate time
2 hours

Route terrain
Riverside and
marshland paths

P **Parking**
Car park at Stodmarsh
Nature Reserve

Dog friendly
Dogs are not permitted
on the nature trail

OS maps
Landranger 179
(Canterbury & East
Kent), Explorer 150
(Canterbury & the Isle
of Thanet)

GPS waypoints
TR 221 609
Ⓐ TR 221 620
Ⓑ TR 235 631
Ⓒ TR 226 617

Stodmarsh and the Stour Valley

An easy, level walk that takes you into the Stodmarsh Nature Reserve and along the banks of the River Great Stour. Hides tucked away off the grassy marshland paths allow you the opportunity to relax and observe close-up the abundant birdlife that inhabits the reed beds and open water. Bring your binoculars and a field guide and allow time to linger along the nature trail.

Stodmarsh Nature Reserve

Hidden away in the peaceful Stour Valley, Stodmarsh Nature Reserve covers a square mile of internationally important reed beds, fens, ditches, wet grassland and open water, which provide one of England's most diverse wetland habitats for breeding and wintering birds, invertebrates and rare plants. Keen birdwatchers should bring their binoculars and spend time in the hides along the nature trail, for Stodmarsh is especially important for birds like the bittern, the marsh harrier and, in summer, for migrant warblers, which flourish in the largest reed bed in South East England.

The earliest recorded use of the land was by Augustinian monks, who dug ditches to encourage floodwater on to the meadows on which they grazed their horses. The marsh provided good grazing for mares in foal and the area was once known as Stud-marsh. Over the years the landscape has changed. In the 17th century in order to prevent flooding, Flemish refugees in the Grove Ferry area built a defence barrier, known as the Lampen Wall. However, in the 20th century Chislet Colliery workings caused the land to subside and become waterlogged once more.

Join the footpath beyond the toilets and information shelter in the top left-hand corner of the car park, passing beside the gate to enter Stodmarsh Nature Reserve. Follow the track right, where a path on the left leads to the Reedbed Hide, then bear left and keep straight on at a junction of paths by a bench.

The track follows the Lampen Wall, passing lakes and ponds to the left and, to the right, you can savour the views across reedbeds and lush grazing marsh. The track narrows beyond Tower Hide, the meandering path soon curving right to reach the River Great Stour Ⓐ.

Remain on this riverside path (can be muddy), with great views across the reserve and Stour Valley, to reach a gate and road opposite the **Grove Ferry Inn** ⓑ. Turn right along the verge for 50 yds and go through the gate on the right to pass Stodmarsh Nature Reserve information boards. The waymarked path cuts across the centre of the reserve, firstly through rough grazing land, passing a mound with benches and a viewpoint that looks across pools, scrapes and marshland – a good vantage point for birdwatchers.

The path then cuts through reed beds, passing Feast's Hide to reach a junction with a footpath leading to Harrison's Drove Hide. Turn right, then immediately left through a kissing-gate to follow the path beside a ditch and across a rough grazing meadow to a footbridge by an information board. Cross the footbridge, then ignore the footbridge on the left and continue on the main path, soon to cross a track via gates.

Pass Marsh Hide on the right and turn sharp left ⓒ to follow the path across a sluice gate and head towards Newborns Farm. On reaching a footbridge on the left, veer sharp right with the path along the edge of the reserve. Pass beside woodland and Undertrees Farm, away to your left, to reach a junction of paths on entering woodland. Turn left across the footbridge and follow the path as it

The River Great Stour

meanders through marshy woodland back to the car park. ●

SCALE 1:25000 or 2½ INCHES to 1 MILE 4CM to 1KM

walk 4

Start
Brookland

Distance
5 miles (8km)

Height gain
Negligible

Approximate time
2 hours

Route terrain
Field paths, country lanes

P Parking
Village hall car park or roadside parking in Brookland

OS maps
Landranger 189 (Ashford & Romney Marsh), Explorer 125 (Romney Marsh, Rye & Winchelsea)

GPS waypoints
TQ 988 257
Ⓐ TQ 974 256
Ⓑ TQ 966 264
Ⓒ TQ 975 246

Brookland and Fairfield

Two fascinating 13th-century Romney Marsh churches are the focus of this atmospheric low-level walk through sheep-filled pastures, open arable fields, across dykes and along quiet lanes. St Augustine's Church in Brookland has a unique detached bell tower and a rare leaden font, and magical Thomas a Becket Church at Fairfield stands isolated in a sheep-grazed field – both are well worth visiting.

From the village hall car park turn left along the lane and cross the stile on the right, just before the Boormans Lane road sign. Keep right along the paddock edge to a stile in the corner and continue alongside a line of trees, bearing diagonally right at the end of the trees across the field to a stile. Join the narrow fenced path that leads to the A259.

Cross to the pavement opposite, turn left and climb the stile on the right into a field. Bear half-left to a gap in the trees, with a yellow-topped post soon coming into view. Maintain direction across the next field to cross a footbridge over a ditch. Turn left beside the ditch, then right at a marker post to follow the footpath beside a hedge on the right to reach a road. Turn left to a T-junction and turn right to pass Harvey Farm on the left, the road soon curving left beside a wall (Poplar Hall right) to a junction with King Street Ⓐ.

A marker post here indicates a path into a large field. Strike out across the field, passing between telegraph poles, heading towards the left-hand of two corrugated barns at Old Farm to cross a stile beyond the farm drive. Go across the footbridge ahead and bear right through the field to a stile close to a green shed. Continue through fields, passing Haywards Farm on the right to reach a footbridge and the road. You now have an uninterrupted view of Fairfield church, isolated in a glorious marshland location. Cross the footbridge opposite and wend

> **Fairfield church** In a truly magical spot, set in a field and surrounded by water courses and sheep, the isolated church of St Thomas a Becket dates from the 13th-century, its ancient timber frame being encased in brickwork and its immense roof covered in red tiles during the 18th century. Stepping inside is like going back in time as the Georgian interior has changed little for over 200 years. Close the heavy door behind you, and all is peaceful and silent, except for the muffled sound of the wind.

your way across grazing pasture via footbridges to the church **B**.

Cross the footbridge beyond the church and follow the raised path to a gate and road. Turn left and keep to the narrow and relatively quiet marshland road, passing The Limes and Dean Court Farm, and eventually reach the A259 **C**.

Cross over, turn right and walk along the verge for 300 yds, bearing off left at the sharp right bend to follow the lane past **The Woolpack**.

> **The Woolpack** Originally a beacon keeper's cottage dating from 1410 and a pub for over 400 years, the Woolpack oozes atmosphere and charm. It was a well-known smuggling haunt when gangs would use the Romney Marsh coast to trade wool for rum and brandy brought over from France.

As the lane bears right, take the arrowed path left down into a field and go through the gate ahead. Bear diagonally right towards a cottage, crossing a ditch and passing in front of the cottage to a stile. Climb the stile, turn right for a few paces along a lane, then cross the stile on the left and walk along the left-hand field edge. Cross a footbridge, walk across the next field to join a lane at the end of fencing. Follow Clubbs Lane to a T-junction, turn right and then left along a grassy path leading to a footbridge and enter the churchyard at Brookland. The ancient Church of St Augustine, with its curious detached wooden belfry tower, is one of the most attractive and interesting churches on Romney Marsh. A visit will reveal a Georgian pulpit and pews and a famous circular lead font. Turn left at the road, then left again past the **Royal Oak** to return to the village hall. ●

SCALE 1:25000 or 2½ INCHES to 1 MILE 4CM to 1KM

Appledore and the Royal Military Canal

Start
Appledore

Distance
5¼ miles (8.4km)

Height gain
180 feet (55m)

Approximate time
2½ hours

Route terrain
Field paths and canal bank

Parking
Car park behind village hall

OS maps
Landranger 189 (Ashford & Romney Marsh), Explorer 125 (Romney Marsh, Rye and Winchelsea)

GPS waypoints
TQ 955 296
Ⓐ TQ 955 297
Ⓑ TQ 959 305
Ⓒ TQ 963 309
Ⓓ TQ 969 317
Ⓔ TQ 974 321

The outward section of this walk follows field paths to the isolated church at Kenardington. The route then reaches the Royal Military Canal and the return follows its bank, with far-ranging views over the marshes and the opportunity of spotting a good variety of birdlife. The Canal was dug in 1804 when Britain feared invasion by Napoleon.

Turn left on the road from the village hall then take the path (Saxon Shore Way) by the public toilets on the recreation ground Ⓐ which crosses diagonally to the opposite corner. Go through a gate and turn left on to the field edge, with council houses to the left. When a hedge meets the path at right angles from the left, bear right to cross the field diagonally, heading for a large oak tree in the far corner. Cross the footbridge here, and cross diagonally the narrow field which follows, to reach a gate. Then cross a large field, heading towards the tumulus at the top. To the left are the chimneys of Hornes Place.

At the top of the field Ⓑ keep right along the field edge, beside a line of oaks to the left. Bear half left across the next field, keeping the power lines well to the right and reaching the lower corner of the field below telegraph lines. Pass through the

St Mary's Church, Kenardington

Map labels (clockwise/as visible):

Silcock's Wood · 42 · Great Heron Wood · Sly Corner · Saxon Shore Way · **E** · Little Heron Wood · Rushfield Wood · 39 · Barricote · **D** · Smith's Farm · Park Wood · Butness Wood · The Firs · Higham Farm · Rentlands · Sheepfolds · Park Hill · Vault · 24 · Thrift Cottage · Oakhouse Farm · **C** · 31 · RMC Path · Kennels · Gusbourne Farm · Hornes Place Chapel · CP · Sheep Wash · Appledore Heath · 26 · **B** · 96 · 97 · 98 · Mill Farm · The Homestead · 8 · 3 · 30 · Magpie Farm · 7 · **A** · Rawnie Farm · Royal Military Road (Track) · P 5 · PO · Appledore · Court Lodge · Appledore Bridge · Mill Mound · Bridge Farm · 29 · Way · Priory Lands · B 2080 · Royal Military · Canal · Blackwater's Arm · The · riffin Farm · 13 · B 2080

SCALE 1:26315 or 2½ INCHES to 1 MILE 3.8CM to 1KM

0 200 400 600 800 METRES 1
KILOMETRES
MILES
0 200 400 600 YARDS ½

gap in the hedge **C**, continue in the same direction across the following field and cross a ditch by a plank bridge. Walk diagonally across the next field to reach the road.

Cross the road into a vineyard, heading for an electric pole, to reach an opening on the far side flanked by trees. Cross the sunken track, climbing steps up the bank on the other side. A small paddock follows, and then a gate and a fence. Now keep the hedge close to the right and when it ends **D** continue in the same direction to reach a corner

after about 100 yds where two hedges meet by a fence corner. Keep the hedge to the right again, continuing on the Saxon Shore Way. Keep ahead to a kissing-gate standing in front of fir trees, with Kenardington church to the left. Almost directly across a road there is a concrete footpath sign. Pass through the gate beside it and follow the edge of the field round to the churchyard where there is another gate **E**.

Head south-eastwards from the churchyard gate **E**, making for a point midway between the two prominent pylons on the skyline. The footpath meets the road before the end of the field opposite Higham Farm, where there is a plank over the ditch. Turn left on the road then right after Higham Farm to walk along the embankment with the Royal Military Canal on the left. Stay by the canal to reach the road at Appledore Bridge. Turn right to return to Appledore, whose history is outlined on a board outside the churchyard.

Sutton Valence and Ulcombe

Start
Sutton Valence

Distance
5¼ miles (8.4km)

Height gain
395 feet (120m)

Approximate time
2½ hours

Route terrain
Field paths, farmland
tracks and quiet
country roads

Parking
On-street at Sutton
Valence

OS maps
Landranger 188
(Maidstone & Royal
Tunbridge Wells),
Explorer 137 (Ashford)

GPS waypoints
TQ 814 492
Ⓐ TQ 821 486
Ⓑ TQ 833 489
Ⓒ TQ 846 497

Sutton Valence stands on the side of the greensand escarpment overlooking the Low Weald. The view of the village from the ridge above at the end of the walk, with the red-tiled roofs in the foreground, gives the scenery of Kent a French feel. The outward part of the walk is on field paths along the lower slopes of the escarpment with the return route following the Greensand Way along the top of the ridge.

The walk starts in the centre of Sutton Valence at the junction of Broad Street and Chapel Road in front of the church that is now used as an arts centre. Facing the former church, turn right and walk down the short lane, turning left at the bottom on to Rectory Lane. A cobbled footpath to the left above the lane climbs and curves round below the scant remains of the castle.

Continue along the lane and bear right by the drive to Cherry Hill on to a lane bearing a 'no through road' sign which passes Sutton Place, on the right, and the first of several orchards. Keep straight on when the surfaced road bends to the right downhill, going down a short length of muddy track to pass College Farm. Beyond this the track is surfaced and, at a T-junction opposite Boyton Court, turn right and walk down the lane. Where it swings sharply left, go across the stile on the left Ⓐ and join a field-edge path with wide views to the right.

Pass through a stile and gateway and to the left of a large pond to reach a stile and a lane above Hecton Farm. Turn left for a few paces before crossing the stile on the right, and follow another field-edge path. Drop down to pass below the retaining wall of a lake and cross the outlet stream to enter a

Sutton Valence

wood, which can be muddy. After the wood cross a field to the iron gate opposite and then head for the lower end of a line of trees ahead **B**. Follow the fence to a stile at the right corner of the field.

Climb a stile on the other side of the lane to reach another field-edge path, which descends to cross a stream by a plank bridge and then walk over the small meadow beyond to reach another lane. Cross this on to a grassy track and soon Ulcombe comes into view as the path skirts a wood. Near the corner of the field, after the wood, the path crosses a ditch on the right and reaches Ulcombe by the primary school. Turn

SCALE 1:25 000 or 2½ INCHES to 1 MILE 4CM to 1KM

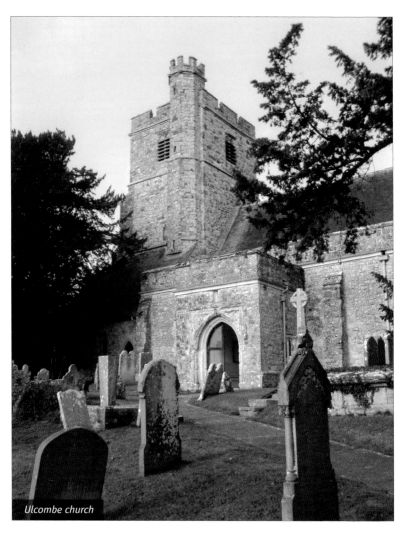
Ulcombe church

left and walk up the village street to reach the church at the top, which has exceptional medieval wall paintings.

Turn left off the road at the church **C** on to the Greensand Way, which passes to the left of a farmyard. When the track reaches a lane at Morry House turn left for 100 yds to find a bridleway sign pointing right through a gate. Keep close to the fence on the right, pass through a gate and walk across the top of a sheltered combe to reach Charlton Lane. Follow Church Lane opposite and pass East Sutton Prison and church.

Cross over Workhouse Road to the stile opposite and then walk across a narrow meadow and the larger field beyond, heading for its distant left-hand corner to reach a crossroads. Turn right into Sutton Valence, but turn off it to the right when a lane joins from the left, following the Greensand Way along a footpath above the road and through the playing field of Sutton Valence school. There is a grand view across the village and The Weald from here. Near the end of the playing field turn left down a flight of steps, which leads to the village centre by the **Swan Inn**, adjacent to the starting point. ●

Westerham and Chartwell

This walk passes Chartwell, country home of Sir Winston Churchill, one of Westerham's two heroes (the other is General Wolfe who was born in the vicarage here). The beginning and end of the route are through the park of Squerryes Court.

walk 7

Start
Westerham church

Distance
5¼ miles (8.4km)

Height gain
705 feet (215m)

Approximate time
2½ hours

Route terrain
Field paths and woodland trails

P Parking
Main car park (Pay and Display) off A25 on east side of town. A footpath leads to the church

OS maps
Landrangers 187 (Dorking & Reigate) and 188 (Maidstone & Royal Tunbridge Wells), Explorer 147 (Sevenoaks & Tonbridge)

GPS waypoints
 TQ 447 540
 A TQ 446 538
 B TQ 445 520
 C TQ 445 515
 D TQ 450 515
 E TQ 453 518
 F TQ 458 528
 G TQ 450 529
 H TQ 448 532

 From the church gates walk across the Green past the statue of Churchill. On the south side of the Green, take a narrow passageway called Water Lane and descend to cross bridges over two streams. Go through a kissing-gate leading into a meadow, and where the footpath divides **A** take the right-hand fork which follows the stream bank.

Go through a kissing-gate and cross a footbridge (part of the Greensand Way) to reach a lane opposite a large pond. Turn left and walk up to the half-timbered Park Lodge. The footpath which continues to the left of the lodge is an enclosed path which climbs steadily; it can become muddy after wet weather.

The enclosed section soon ends and then the path crosses two parkland meadows, passing through a clump of trees in the second to a farm track. Turn left on to this and descend steadily into a wooded valley. Keep straight on at a junction at the bottom to reach a stile by an iron gate. Climb the stile and follow the path gently round the edge of a wood on the right, enjoying changing views of the valley. The trees to the right

The Churchill statue at Westerham

recede to reveal a beautifully situated white house.

A stile **B** takes the footpath into the woods close to Crockham House, and here it splits into three. Take the middle path, which climbs steeply up through rhododendrons. At the top of the hill **C** turn left on to a bridleway, then first left again and head steeply downhill. Join the Greensand Way and the drive from April Cottage at the bottom and follow this up to the road.

Cross the road to a bridleway opposite which climbs to reach a footpath at the top by two magnificent beeches. The Greensand Way leaves to the left here **D**, but the route continues ahead, with a paling fence to the right, to cross the drive to Windmill Bank. Trees partly screen the fine views to the right as the bridleway descends to the road at Chartwell. Turn left on to this to pass Churchill's home. The back of the house is seen from the road – *take care as there are no footpaths*. Farther on are views of the surrounding park.

Leave the road to the right, just after the entrance to the car park **E**, rejoining the Greensand Way which climbs steeply on the edge of the Chartwell estate. Cross straight over the road at the top and continue on the bridleway, following it to the road at French Street where there is a property on the right called Mannings Wood. Turn left (the Greensand Way leaves to the right) and climb the road to pass a cemetery on the right. Just after this turn on to a tarmac drive on the left marked by a footpath waymark **F**. A path leaves the drive to the right opposite Brackenwood.

The route is now on a very pleasant woodland path which winds through bracken and pine trees at first and then enters more densely planted timber. It eventually reaches a car park at Hosey Hill. Walk to the road at the top end of the car park, turn left along it to a public footpath sign and follow this right, to the left of stables which have a miniature castellated tower.

The path twists through woodland and eventually meets another footpath which runs along the edge of a planting of conifers **G**. Turn right on to this tree-lined path which descends steadily and finally reaches a gate at the bottom of the wood **H**. After the gate turn right and climb a steep bank with fine oaks

The Green at Westerham

and beeches to the right. At the top the tower of Westerham church can be seen straight ahead but the line of the footpath lies to the left of this and is plainly visible on the ground. Follow this as it drops down through a parkland meadow and cross a stile before reaching the gate at the end of Water Lane which was encountered earlier, and continue back to the starting point.

SCALE 1:25000 or 2½ INCHES to 1 MILE 4CM to 1KM

walk 8

Start
Sandwich

Distance
6 miles (9.6km)

Height gain
Negligible

Approximate time
2½ hours

Route terrain
Rough grassland and field paths, coastal track, tarmac paths

P Parking
The Quay car park (Pay and Display) in Sandwich

OS maps
Landranger 179 (Canterbury & East Kent), Explorer 150 (Canterbury & the Isle of Thanet)

GPS waypoints
- TR 332 582
- Ⓐ TR 356 592
- Ⓑ TR 361 581
- Ⓒ TR 346 568

Sandwich and Sandwich Bay

From the historic Cinque Port of Sandwich this easy, level walk follows the River Stour before heading across rough pasture to the breezy shores of Sandwich Bay. The return route crosses famous Royal St George's Golf Course, which has hosted numerous Open Championships, and passes through Sandwich Bay Nature Reserve. Take your binoculars and visit the bird observatory to find out the day's migrant sightings.

Sandwich Exuding great charm and character, Sandwich is the oldest Cinque Port and stands on the River Stour, though the sea is now 2 miles away. Reminders of the Flemish weavers, who landed in Kent at the end of the 16th century, abound in the form of superb timbered houses and inns that can be seen in the town. The Barbican, a medieval conical-towered gate, and Fishergate remain and other notable buildings include St Clement's Church, which has a fine Norman tower and displays carvings of the same period, and the Old House is a fine Tudor building.

Head east on a traffic-free tarmac road, parallel with the River Stour, away from the town. On nearing houses, bear left across a footbridge to join a narrow surfaced path that affords good river views. Keep left at the fork of paths to follow the meandering tarmac path close to the river.

Eventually, cross a sluice gate to reach the road and bear left for a few paces to cross the waymarked stile on the right. Follow the defined path across rough grassland to reach a stile. Do not cross the stile, instead, walk beside the fencing, following it left before bearing diagonally right with the good path, heading across grassland towards the right-hand edge of a line of fir trees. At the trees, go through the kissing-gate and continue towards buildings, with St George's Golf Course to the right and good views left to Ramsgate. Merge with a track coming in from the left and follow it to the coast road at Sandwich Bay **Ⓐ**.

Turn right, then at the car park and toilets, bear left to join a track that heads south close to the pebble beach.

SCALE 1:25000 or 2½ INCHES to 1 MILE *4CM to 1KM*

Sandwich Bay

The Saxon Shore Way

Cross the railway with care, go through a gate and follow the track ahead, which soon becomes surfaced at Blue Pigeons Farm. Turn right at a sharp left bend, just beyond Temptye Farmhouse, to follow a bridleway along a tarmac drive. At a crossing of paths by a white cottage, turn right on to a reed-fringed tarmac path that leads to a footbridge over a stream. Still metalled, the path heads across the field, then parallel to a ditch to pass a nursery on the left to reach a road.

Turn right along the pavement, go over the railway crossing and pass St George's Road before turning right along Mill Wall, a tarmac footpath that follows the Old Town Walls (Saxon Shore Way). With cameo views across the town, follow this to a road and cross over to walk beside the perimeter fence to The Salutation (Secret Gardens), bearing left back to The Quay and car park. ●

Pass more toilets and ignore the arrowed path (right) across the golf course. Continue towards Sandwich Bay Estate to locate another path on the right **Ⓑ**.

Go through the kissing-gate and follow the white-painted and yellow-topped marker posts across the golf course to reach a stile. Walk across meadows via gates to reach a tarmac byway (Guilford Road). Cross over and walk down the driveway to Sandwich Bay Bird Observatory. Call into the observatory for refreshments and to view the blackboard detailing current sightings. Remain on the track, the bridleway soon bearing left to follow close to a reed-fringed stream. Where it veers sharp left, bear off right and soon cross a bridge over the stream to join a narrow, high-hedged path that leads to a gate and a railway crossing **Ⓒ**.

> ### Secret Gardens
> The Secret Gardens at The Salutation, a Grade I-listed manor house designed by Sir Edwin Lutyens, who also devised the 3½ acres of ornamental gardens, are an oasis of calm and are surrounded by the old city walls. After lying neglected for 25 years, the White Garden and the Bowling Green have been recreated and new features, like the Tropical Border, have been added.

Sissinghurst Castle garden

| **Start** |
| Farthing Common |

| **Distance** |
| 5½ miles (8km) |

| **Height gain** |
| 820 feet (250m) |

| **Approximate time** |
| 3 hours |

| **Route terrain** |
| Downland paths and tracks |

| **Parking** |
| Farthing Common car park |

| **OS maps** |
| Landranger 179 (Canterbury & East Kent) and Explorer 138 (Dover, Folkestone & Hythe) |

| **GPS waypoints** |
| TR 136 403 |
| Ⓐ TR 145 393 |
| Ⓑ TR 154 393 |
| Ⓒ TR 160 387 |
| Ⓓ TR 157 380 |
| Ⓔ TR 147 385 |
| Ⓕ TR 145 391 |

Farthing Common, Postling and Tolsford Hill

This route is a delight, especially the opening section which is reversed for the return. Here steep-sided valleys are concealed below the crest of the downs, with grassy paths threaded through. The walking is often energetic but on a clear day the views are outstanding.

At the road junction on the south side of the car park, turn left along the lane away from the B-road. Just before the next junction, follow the North Downs Way sign right along the left-hand edge of a field, soon to keep left with the field boundary, heading towards radio masts.

The path leads to a kissing-gate overlooking a dry valley. Take the path down into the steep-sided valley, following the waymarks until you reach a gate where another path joins from the right. The path now swings left, climbing a grassy defile. Turn right at the fence at the top, the path soon swinging sharply left to reveal Postling church before dropping from the crest of the downs on to a ledge, which curves around another U-shaped combe. At the southern end of the combe climb steeply to a gate Ⓐ.

Follow the path along the field edge ahead to a gate, then drop down the field to a stile and gate, passing under power lines as you go. Cross the stile and walk down the field to a waymark in the bottom boundary. Bear left along the hedge, parallel with the road, and make for a gate in the field corner by Staple Farm Ⓑ.

Cross the road, bearing slightly to the right, following the North Downs Way to a gate. Climb the steep slope of the downs close to a fence. The top of the radio mast ahead can be seen and the whole structure is revealed as you near the summit.

At the fence, bear left and follow it, with the two transmitters on the right, to pass through a gate. Still keeping the transmitters on your right, make for the stile ahead, cross the small field beyond to another stile and join a concrete track. At the second left bend, veer off right on to a grassy track Ⓒ to follow it south towards a triangulation pillar at the summit of Tolsford Hill. After the pillar it descends steeply through a

narrow
defile, passing
through several
gates before
reaching a crossing
of paths **D**.

Turn right on to a
bridleway, part of the
Pilgrim's Way. Keep
fairly close to the
fence at the bottom of
the downs to reach the
south corner of Tolsford
Plantation. Go round the edge of the
spinney, then keep the fence to the right
and continue to the road.

Cross the road to Cuckoo Lane
opposite and follow it until you reach a
stile to the left of the drive to Vicarage
Farm on your right **E**. Cross the stile,
walk beside the drive for 50 yds before

Postling church

SCALE 1:31 250 or 2 INCHES to 1 MILE 3.2CM to 1KM

bearing half-left to cross the meadow
and reach another stile by an electricity
post. Climb this stile and the following
one close by in the next paddock, and
turn right to follow the hedgerow to a
cross a stile in the field corner. Head
towards the church, go through a gate
and bear left to cross a plank bridge
between stiles, and take the path into
Postling.

Turn right along the road, walk past
the church, and then turn left at the
telephone box. Opposite the drive to
Churchfield turn right on to a footpath,
passing through a gate **F** and climbing
up a steep grassy path to reach the top
of the escarpment, and the North Downs
Way, just below **A**. Repeat the lovely
section walked at the start, back to
Farthing Common.

walk 10

⬤ Start
Lamberhurst

Distance
6 miles (9.6km)

Height gain
720 feet (220m)

⏱ Approximate time
3 hours

Route terrain
Field and woodland paths; section along a country road

P Parking
Car park at Lamberhurst, just off High Street

Dog friendly
Some stiles with no dog gaps

OS maps
Landranger 188 (Maidstone & Royal Tunbridge Wells) and Explorer 136 (High Weald, Royal Tunbridge Wells)

GPS waypoints
⬤ TQ 676 362
Ⓐ TQ 672 357
Ⓑ TQ 666 355
Ⓒ TQ 660 348
Ⓓ TQ 654 359
Ⓔ TQ 661 373
Ⓕ TQ 664 370

Lamberhurst and Hook Green

This walk explores the countryside around the village of Lamberhurst on the western boundary of Kent, and for a few minutes the route cuts across a loop in the border with East Sussex. Just before this there is a view of one of the loveliest scenes of any of these walks as the path drops down to a wood with a lake, traditional oast houses and a farmhouse in the distance.

⬤ Leave the car park, cross the road, and fork right to take the Wadhurst road out of Lamberhurst, climbing the hill as you do so. At the top, just before Sand Road, take the footpath on the right Ⓐ which goes up steps and into a vineyard. There is a fine view to the right with Bayham Abbey in the distance. Follow the path ahead with vineyard buildings, farm shop and café away to your left, and walk beside and between vines for almost ½ mile until eventually you reach a concrete drive. Turn left, go through a former farmyard to reach the road.

Turn left and after a few yards right Ⓑ down a narrow path by the side of the drive to Misty Meadow Farm. After a slightly unpromising start this becomes a delightful field-edge path dropping down towards Owls Castle, where there are oast houses rather than battlements. Enter a wood which borders the lower of three large ponds – a lovely scene with an attractive

Towards Bayham Abbey

farmhouse and oast houses beyond. The path descends to the first of two footbridges, the second of which leads into Sussex. Cross the meadow after a stile, bearing half-left to reach another stile just below a belt of trees. The path runs below these trees above the second and third ponds, climbing steadily towards the top of the valley and eventually following the edge of a field. There is a grand view back.

At the end of the field follow a short length of path enclosed by a stableyard on one side and a holly hedge on the other and after a few yards take the footpath on the right **C** to a field-edge path with a copse to the left. At the end of the copse the path continues in the same direction across a field with a stile

SCALE 1:25000 or 2½ INCHES to 1 MILE 4CM to 1KM

Cottage near Owl House

on the far side. The next field is a meadow bisected by a tiny stream which is the county boundary between Kent and Sussex. Cross this to a stile on to a lane and climb the stile opposite to follow the path by the side of a field and then a wood. At the corner of the wood turn right to keep following its edge; when it ends continue along the edge of two fields. The path meets the road via the drive of Durrants Cottage.

Turn right and walk to the crossroads at Hook Green **D**, with the **Elephant's Head** pub away to your right. Cross the B2169 and follow the road ahead, the narrow country lane soon curving right downhill to cross the River Teise. Pass the converted oast houses of Hoathly Farm and keep left at the road junction to follow Clay Hill Road. A lengthy climb follows with views of a lake below to the right. Opposite the cottages at the top of the hill, at the start of a left-hand bend, take the waymarked track right, which descends through the woods to a gate and a field, with a barn ahead. In a few yards, cross the stile on the right and follow the right-hand field edge, passing a house on the left, and the shore of a lake, before turning left to join a track. After 100 yds turn right

over a footbridge and across a stile. Keep right at the path junction and walk up through a wild meadow, with a white weatherboard house away to your left. Just beyond it, turn right over a stile and climb the steep slope **E**, curving left along the edge of the wood and then out of the trees and between white railings to reach a stile which leads on to the drive to the Owl House.

The famous Owl House Garden is to the left, but to follow the route turn right on to the drive and walk along it for 200 yds to Owl House Fruit Farm. Here **F** take a very narrow, overgrown path leading down by the left side of the house. The path is better when it reaches a field. Continue down to the corner by a tennis court but do not cross the stile. Instead turn right and keep to the edge of two fields – the wood is to the left for much of the way. At the rear of Barnfield Oast take the enclosed path on the left to the road. Take a few steps left to find the continuation of the path on the other side of the road.

The path crosses an open field and when it meets the end of a hedge keep the hedge to the left, but turn left well before the bottom of the field, at the point where another hedge joins from the right. This path heads across the field to a barn and a track. Bear left past the barn, then cross the stile on the right and over a meadow to a footbridge spanning the River Teise. After this it is but a few steps to Lamberhurst. Turn left at the road to return to the car park. ●

Knole Park, Godden Green and One Tree Hill

walk 11

Start
One Tree Hill, near Sevenoaks

Distance
6 miles (9.5km)

Height gain
705 feet (215m)

Approximate time
3 hours

Route terrain
Parkland paths and woodland trails

Parking
National Trust car park at One Tree Hill

Dog friendly
Dogs must be kept on leads through Knole Park

OS maps
Landranger 188 (Maidstone & Royal Tunbridge Wells), Explorer 147 (Sevenoaks & Tonbridge)

GPS waypoints
TQ 558 531
Ⓐ TQ 552 530
Ⓑ TQ 535 543
Ⓒ TQ 540 544
Ⓓ TQ 552 551
Ⓔ TQ 557 546
Ⓕ TQ 567 541
Ⓖ TQ 565 538

Almost half this walk is within Knole's magnificent deer park. There are good views of the house itself, which was built in the 15th century and enlarged in 1603 by the first Earl of Dorset. The route returns over the top of the ridge and the famous viewpoint of One Tree Hill.

From the car park, keep left of the information board and pass through fencing to follow the wide path ahead through the trees. At a T-junction, turn right and follow the path down to the road. Turn left then at the corner, leave the road, turning right on to the drive to Shepherds Mead. Turn off before the white gate, following the Greensand Way sign, on to an enclosed path, first by a garden fence and then beside a field with a wood to the right. At a track go right and then left over a stile to cross a track at the end of the woods Ⓐ and enter a large field with steeple-chase jumps. The path crosses to the far right-hand corner (but most walkers go round the edge) to a stile and enters an old birch wood and soon reaches a lane. An entrance to the deer park is opposite.

Go through the gate on to a path, with the deer fence to the right. Go straight across Chestnut Walk and onto a surfaced track, which ends at a T-junction. The route continues straight ahead along a grassy, then sandy, track which soon brings Knole into view. The path follows Knole's garden wall, and the house can be seen through wrought-iron railings.

Opposite the west corner of the house the path becomes less distinct and bears slightly left to drop down through a group of trees to join a tarmac path to the main drive Ⓑ. Turn right on to this and bear left when it divides. A path crosses soon after and just over the brow of the hill there is a crossroads with the main drive bending to the right towards the house. Keep straight on here along a tarmac drive which soon meets another which passes through an avenue of oaks. Turn left to go through the trees Ⓒ.

The track crosses a golf course and climbs the slope on the other side to the hill top at Godden Wood, where it leaves Knole.

Keep on the sandy track after the gate through the deer fence; it passes through rhododendrons as it crosses heathland. Fork right on to a narrow, sandy path when the track divides and pass between two bungalows. Cross straight over a lane by stables to reach Godden Green by the **Buck's Head** pub Ⓓ.

Turn right and walk southwards along the green, then bear left away from the road on a lane to 'Cygnet Hospital Godden Green' past the White House. After the hospital the lane becomes a rough bridleway. About 120 yds past Damson Mead a footpath branches off to the right; continue for a few more paces and fork right on to a second footpath at a concrete marker Ⓔ.

Go up the bank here into Lord's Spring Wood. Cross straight over two paths and then follow the path down a deeply etched defile to a stile on to a field. Cross to the right-hand side of a finger of woodland about 120 yds from the stile. Now join a roughly enclosed path on your right, and continue beside a wire fence

Knole Park

and over the next stile. Climb the narrow path through the woods, bearing left to continue the climb as you pass a tennis court to the right. The path reaches a drive leading to a road **F**.

Turn right on to the road, which soon drops down, swings to the right, and then levels out. In the middle of the level stretch take the signposted footpath which branches off to the left **G** and fork left when it divides. The path climbs steadily through woodland and when it meets another path at the top turn left. Turn right when this reaches a lane.

Walk past High Orchard and take the bridleway which drops down to the right of the ball-topped gateposts of Rooks Hill House on the left. The steep descent ends at the lane which goes to Rooks Hill Cottage. Look to the right when you reach the lane to see steps which take the Greensand Way up to recapture the height just lost. A splendid stretch of walking follows along the crest of Rooks Hill to a stile, into the National Trust's One Tree Hill estate. Continue to the granite bench on One Tree Hill, where you leave the Greensand Way and fork right to return to the car park. ●

SCALE 1:26000 or 2½ INCHES to 1 MILE 4CM to 1KM

walk 12

Mereworth Woods and West Peckham

Start	Mereworth church
Distance	6¼ miles (10km)
Height gain	655 feet (200m)
Approximate time	3 hours
Route terrain	Orchard paths and woodland trails
Parking	On-road in Mereworth
OS maps	Landranger 188 (Maidstone & Royal Tunbridge Wells), Explorer 148 (Maidstone & the Medway Towns)

GPS waypoints

- TQ 660 537
- Ⓐ TQ 657 538
- Ⓑ TQ 642 538
- Ⓒ TQ 631 539
- Ⓓ TQ 629 536
- Ⓔ TQ 631 529
- Ⓕ TQ 629 524
- Ⓖ TQ 641 524
- Ⓗ TQ 640 532

This invigorating walk uses an attractive part of the Wealdway, climbing through Hurst Wood and returning by West Peckham, where church and pub beside the village green make a perfect picture if cricket is being played. After this there is a climb to the top of the Wealden ridge before the return to Mereworth.

Starting with your back to the church, walk left along the village street for about 150 yds to Torrington House on the right. Immediately after, along the side of the house, turn right along a little lane to a narrow enclosed path which has an orchard to the right. Very soon another narrow path leaves to the right Ⓐ. Take this and climb up to join a driveway from a large white house which reaches a lane on a sharp bend. Keep straight on here and bear left at the next road junction, with Horns Lane. There are good views back to Mereworth as you approach the following junction, with New Pound Lane. Keep ahead here to reach the main road and go directly across to the footpath opposite. This follows a farm track, with adjacent fields of fruit bushes under polytunnels.

Turn left when the track reaches a lane and then right after a pond to walk up another track, passing in front of a cottage to reach a gate. Enter a meadow and make for the edge of Hurst Wood Ⓑ. Bear right at the edge of the wood and follow the track

Mereworth church

left beside the wood in a few paces.

The right of way is a humble, often muddy, track which climbs steadily up a valley to reach a vast coppice of beech and ash trees. Keep straight on when another path crosses, continuing the steady climb.

Turn left at the next track **C**, just below the summit and before a gate. There is one beech tree remaining with convoluted roots. The path, now level, soon reaches a further crossways. Go straight over here but turn left at the next crossing **D** on to a broader track heading south. Cross straight over a lane, following the Wealdway logo, to a path above another lane. This is Gover

SCALE 1:26315 or 2⅖ INCHES to 1 MILE 3.8CM to 1KM

West Peckham church

Hill, the small sector of Mereworth Woods owned by the National Trust. Soon the path descends to reach the road **E**.

Cross straight over this complex junction to a track to the left of a white cottage. Just before the track reaches the trees at the bottom look for a Wealdway sign pointing to the left **F** into an orchard. Keep right, along the edge of the orchard, the path swinging right at the far end to join a farm track.

The track meets the road at East Lodge. Turn left and then look for the white railings to the right where the footpath runs above the lane, and parallel to it for a short distance to a gate. A little farther on the path leaves the lane, bearing to the south-east with a row of poplars to the left and an orchard beyond as it heads down towards a house **G**. Go through a gate and cross the drive to head towards the tower of West Peckham church, emerging on to the beautiful village green with **The Swan on the Green** pub at one corner and the church at another. Continue eastwards from the church

and turn left into Forge Lane towards Plaxtol. Fork right into Stan Lane when the lane divides and climb to the top of this quiet byway, passing to the left of Beech Farm.

The lane begins to level out at a modern house on the left. Opposite this house **H** turn into a bridleway on the right, which soon descends out of the trees to afford wonderful views. After a row of trees ends you can see Mereworth Castle in the distance ahead – a rare glimpse of this private house. The path swings around a house and the unusual spire of Mereworth church comes into view. It then skirts the rear of Yotes Court, swinging to the right to approach the farmyard. Just beyond a cottage with pointed windows on the left, turn left on to a muddy track which passes cattlesheds on the other side of a hedge to the right.

This track narrows and then skirts a spinney before reaching the road by a renovated gate-lodge. Turn left, cross over the main road into Mereworth and continue along the street back to the church. ●

Egerton and Pluckley

walk 13

Orchard, field and farmland paths lead through Kent's 'Garden of England' landscape to Pluckley, reputedly England's most haunted village and made famous in the TV series The Darling Buds of May, *which was filmed around the village. The return route to Egerton explores the Greensand Way, with its glorious views across the Weald and the North Downs.*

Start	Egerton
Distance	6¾ miles (10.8km)
Height gain	360 feet (110m)
Approximate time	3 hours
Route terrain	Orchard and field paths and bridleways
Parking	Egerton Village Hall, at the end of Elm Close
OS maps	Landranger 189 (Ashford & Romney Marsh), Explorer 137 (Ashford)
GPS waypoints	TQ 906 473
	A TQ 924 469
	B TQ 944 458
	C TQ 926 454
	D TQ 912 461

> **Egerton** Egerton stands on the top of the Greensand ridge with far-reaching views across the Weald of Kent. It's a thriving community, the focus being the 13th-century church, the George Inn and the impressive village hall, which hosts a local farmers' market every Friday.

Go up the steps opposite the children's play area on to the village street and turn right towards the **George Inn**. Turn right before the pub along New Road, signed to Pluckley. Just as you leave the village, climb the stile on the left, opposite Stone Hill Road. Cross the field to a stile and walk ahead through the orchard, then bear slightly right across an open field, looking for a gap in the hedge to reach a footpath crossing. Climb the stile ahead, cut right across the field corner to a stile and bear diagonally left over a large field to join a farm track to the right of Iden Farm Cottage and turn right.

Walk beside woodland, soon to merge with the Stour Valley Walk (SVW) to reach a road **A**. Turn right for a few paces, then left to follow another field-edge track (Nettlepole Lane). On reaching Little Pipers Wood, take the waymarked path left diagonally through the wood. Exit the trees and walk straight across the field to join a track in the field corner, which takes you along a line of poplar trees to a stile and road.

Turn left, then cross over at Chart Court Farm, noting the striking painted cowls on the oast house, to follow the SVW through a churchyard, passing the ruins of St Mary's Church. Join a concrete driveway, the track soon bearing left in front of barns and passing between paddocks to eventually enter a

> **H E Bates** The author H E Bates, who wrote *The Darling Buds of May*, which was made into a TV series and filmed in the area starring David Jason as Pop Larkin, lived in Little Chart from 1931 until his death in 1974.

field. Turn left and follow the field edge beside trees and cross the iron footbridge on the left by a mill house. The narrow surfaced path leads you round Ford Mill into Little Chart.

Turn right along the road to a junction by the **Swan Inn**. Turn left and almost immediately climb the steps on your right **B** into rough grassland, with Little Chart church away to your left. Follow the defined path, now the Greensand Way (GW), to enter an orchard beyond a track. Keep to the GW as it meanders gently uphill through apple orchards. Exit the orchards via an enclosed path beside a vineyard, soon to walk beside a brick wall to reach a lane. Cross over and continue walking through orchards, passing in front of Sheerland Farm, to eventually cross a playing field into Pluckley **C**.

| Ghostly Pluckley | Pluckley is reputedly the |

Ghostly Pluckley Pluckley is reputedly the most haunted village in the country, claiming at least twelve ghosts. One such spirit resides at the Black Horse in the form of a poltergeist, while others include a highwayman, a monk, and a Red Lady who is seen wandering through the churchyard.

Go through a gate and turn left downhill through the village. Turn left if you wish to visit the **Black Horse** and the church, otherwise follow the pavement down to a waymarked bridleway on the right (GW), which leads past houses to reach a gate. Walk ahead, pass through two further gates and follow a defined path through two rough pastures, with grand views along the Greensand ridge and across the Weald, heading gently

Egerton

downhill to a gate.

Walk along the field edge, bear right into the adjoining field and follow the left-hand edge to a gate in the hedge. Continue towards the oast at **Elvey Farm** (Hotel & Restaurant) and pass in front of the farmhouse to a crossing of footpaths. Go through the double wooden gates ahead and walk straight across the field ahead to a stile. Cut across the field corner to a further stile, then turn right along the field edge to a stile and farm track **D**.

Turn right through the gate and bear left across the stile beside a gate. Keep close to the left-hand field edge, soon to bear left uphill below Greenhill Farm

to cross a stile on to a lane. Walk uphill, dropping down steps on the left at the right-hand bend. Cross the stile, keep to the high ground, following the fence right to a gate and bear right through the next field, enjoying fabulous Wealden views, to reach a stile and gate.

A concrete track leads up through Stone Hill Farm to Stone Hill Road. Turn right, then in 150 yds, take the arrowed path left and follow the enclosed path back to Egerton Village Hall.

●

SCALE 1:25000 or 2½ INCHES to 1 MILE 4CM to 1KM

walk 14

Ightham Mote and Oldbury Hill

⟋ Start
Ightham Mote

⟰ Distance
6¾ miles (10.8km)

⟰ Height gain
900 feet (275m)

⏱ Approximate time
3½ hours

👢 Route terrain
Orchard paths and woodland trails

P Parking
National Trust car park at Ightham Mote

⟳ OS maps
Landranger 188 (Maidstone & Royal Tunbridge Wells), Explorer 147 (Sevenoaks & Tonbridge)

⊡ GPS waypoints
- ⟋ TQ 584 536
- Ⓐ TQ 583 537
- Ⓑ TQ 570 549
- Ⓒ TQ 573 551
- Ⓓ TQ 575 562
- Ⓔ TQ 583 563
- Ⓕ TQ 581 555
- Ⓖ TQ 578 547

Apart from the early orchard section this is almost entirely a woodland walk, glorious in autumn. In spring the colours are more subtle but no less appealing. Near the end of the walk, there are some good views from Raspit Hill. Allow time to visit historic Ightham Mote, the start point and focus of this walk.

Ightham Mote Ightham Mote is often acclaimed as the most perfect medieval house in England. Dating from the 13th century, it has been extensively restored by the National Trust with some English Heritage funding.

⟋ From the car park walk past the south side of the house, following a bridleway to the road. Turn right and pass old cottages on the right. Note the privies with decorative arches on the other side of the road.

Turn left at the bridleway sign opposite a stone house Ⓐ and pass some old hoppers' huts on the left along a bridleway leading into a wooded valley. The track soon narrows and becomes enclosed by woodland; 150 yds farther on, bear right at the fork and climb to the top. It is steep and can be muddy after rain. At the top is an orchard and the bridleway joins a track between the trees. Cross over a road junction and continue on the bridleway on the other side, now with fruit trees on your right. Follow the well-made track past an attractive stone-built farmhouse, and continue until you reach a road opposite the **Padwell Arms**, Stone Street. Turn right here.

Walk along the road for 150 yds and then turn left Ⓑ along a drive to St Lawrence Vicarage. When the drive divides take

Ightham Mote

the enclosed footpath between the two drives and climb up behind Stone House. Keep straight on when a path leaves to the left. Fallen trees may obscure the path here, but it climbs steadily in a northerly direction through the remaining beech trees. Bear right on the track at the top to reach Church Road and turn right again.

Pass the church and the school. Just after the latter **C** fork left on to the bridleway and walk 100 yds to a gate on the left which is the entrance to a narrow bridleway leading down steeply through the trees. At the bottom is a quiet lane which reaches the main road, the A25, by the **Crown Point Inn**.

Cross the road to the waymarked footpath opposite, and follow it as it winds down through oaks and birches. Turn left when this meets a bridleway, following it up on the left side of a campsite. Almost at the top turn right **D** on to a narrow path, marked by a concrete waymark, which leads down the north side of the campsite to a lane. Turn left and just before Styants Farm House turn right on to a bridleway which climbs up to and passes through a ravine (after wet weather the path is shared with a stream). At the top the walking is through woods with glimpses of open

SCALE 1:31250 or 2 INCHES to 1 MILE 3.2CM to 1KM

Oast houses at Mote Farm

country to the left. This is Oldbury Hill, where there was once an Iron Age fort. The path passes a small pond and soon after this you'll come to a National Trust information board. Just past the board, fork right onto the waymarked byway and continue 130 yds to the next bridleway junction **E**. Turn sharp right and follow the path as it winds on through the woods. Bear left when it meets with another track, walk down a ravine and soon emerge on to the A25.

Rather than follow the busy road to the right, bear right here **F** on to a bridleway which strikes off in a north-westerly direction. This leads to a quiet lane where there is a car park. Turn sharp left down the lane to reach the main road again. To the left across the road is the entrance to a bridleway leading into

Fish Ponds Wood. This is another enjoy-able woodland walk, past the ponds on a sandy track up a valley. The final section climbs a steep flight of wooden steps up to the rim of the valley **G**.

Turn left and bear right at a waymark in a few paces to follow a path close to the edge of the escarpment – there are good views when breaks in the trees allow. It is important to keep close to the edge to find a path which leads down the steep slope to a road. Cross the road to continue on the bridleway opposite. Pass a barn on the left, then an orchard to the right and later the way becomes rocky and somewhat tortuous as the path descends a hill. The bridleway reaches a lane by Mote Hill Cottage. Turn right to return to Ightham Mote.

Benenden and Rolvenden

walk 15

Start
Benenden

Distance
7 miles (11.2km)

Height gain
590 feet (180m)

Approximate time
3½ hours

Route terrain
Field paths, woodland trails, quiet country lanes

Parking
Benenden Village Hall car park

OS maps
Landranger 188 (Maidstone & Royal Tunbridge Wells), Explorer 125 (Romney Marsh, Rye and Winchelsea)

GPS waypoints
🖉 TQ 810 328
Ⓐ TQ 814 315
Ⓑ TQ 831 311
Ⓒ TQ 844 312
Ⓓ TQ 839 326
Ⓔ TQ 827 336

Following the High Weald Landscape Trail, this peaceful rural ramble explores gently rolling countryside between the classic Wealden villages of Benenden and Rolvenden. Set on a high spot of the Weald, Benenden is notable for its glorious village green, with old timbered houses, chestnut trees, a cricket pitch and great pub. In Rolvenden, allow time to visit the church and the quirky and unique C M Booth Motor Museum on the High Street.

🖉 Turn left out of the car park, pass **The Bull** pub and turn left beside the green. Pass the church lychgate, take the track ahead and bear left around the churchyard. At a fork, take the narrow path on the left and walk downhill to the road. Keep to the left verge and climb a stile beyond the drive to Woodside. Bear half-right across the field to the end of the hedgerow ahead, then walk down the left-hand edge to a footbridge and gate and enter Iden Green Wood. Walk through the coppiced woodland, keeping left on merging with another path and follow it down to a stile. Exit the trees, the now fenced path leading to a stile and lane Ⓐ.

Turn left along the quiet lane, soon to bear right at a junction by nurseries, then left at a fork to join a dead-end lane. Soon after the tarmac ends at Dingleden Farm, fork left along the grassy track to pass a tennis court, the track eventually narrowing to reach a stile and gate. Bear diagonally left to where the line of trees end ahead and follow the right-hand field edge to a stile. Pass through a band of trees, cross a stile and turn left along the edge of an orchard. Go through a gap in the far left-hand corner to follow the marked path along the right-hand edge of the next orchard to a gate. Follow the right-hand field edge to another gate and a lane Ⓑ.

Go through the gate opposite, bear half-left towards a lone tree and bear right after it to drop down beside woodland to a stile. Cross a plank bridge, ascend through trees to another stile and follow the right-hand field edge ahead, with Rolvenden Windmill soon coming into view away to your left. This fine old post mill, considered the oldest in Kent, was restored in 1956. Cross a stile, pass through the gate ahead and bear diagonally left to locate a stile in the field corner, between a corrugated barn and Rolvenden church tower. Head towards the church, crossing two fields, then walk along the right-hand field edge, soon to bear right through trees on nearing houses to reach a recreation ground. Keep left to a gate and the A28 in Rolvenden **C**.

> **Rolvenden** A village of tiled and weather-boarded houses, Rolvenden includes a large 14th-century church, which contains a curious upstairs pew, originally meant for the lord of the manor.

Turn left along the pavement and turn left at the junction with the B2086. Cross the road, pass the **Bull Inn** and take the bridleway between the pub car park and a barn. Head north along the hedged track, pass through two gates and descend steeply along the field edge, with views across Hole Park, to reach a gate and woodland. Turn right, then fork left in a few paces to cross a footbridge and climb steeply to a gate. Walk straight on, then head across the field when the woodland to your right ends, to locate a concrete track to the left of Rawlinson Farm. Follow it right, around the farmhouse and turn left just beyond the oast house to pass close to a pond to reach a stile **D**.

Walk down the right-hand field edge, climb a stile and bear left down the field edge to a stile into woodland. Cross two bridges, go up steps and enter a small plantation. Go left at the fence ahead, cross a stile on the right and bear diagonally left across the field to join a track by trees in the field corner. In a few steps, follow the path right uphill beside the trees, bearing left before turning right along a track to a tarmac farm road by Maplesden Farm. Turn left and follow it to the lane.

Turn right, then left across the stile in a few paces and walk down the right-hand field edge to cross the left-hand stile in the field corner at woodland. Cross the footbridge in the valley

SCALE 1:25 000 or 2½ INCHES to 1 MILE 4CM to 1KM

bottom, then climb through the field ahead to a waymarked gate. Continue uphill to locate a stile just to the right of a pond. Cut across the corner of the field to an oak tree and then follow the left-hand field edge to go through double gates to the left of a barn. Turn left at the farm road by Pagehurst Cottage, the tarmac lane giving way to a hedged track at an oast house **E**.

Keep to the wide track as it wends west, passing woodland and ponds on the left, to reach a junction of tracks. Turn left and remain on this track as it curves right through the wooded valley to eventually reach a lane below a cottage. Turn left and follow the road back into Benenden. ●

Wealden view from Benenden

walk 16

Shoreham and Lullingstone Park

Start
Shoreham

Distance
7 miles (11.25km)

Height gain
690 feet (210m)

Approximate time
3½ hours

Route terrain
Field and woodland paths

Parking
Filston Lane car park at south end of Shoreham

Dog friendly
Some stiles without dog-gaps

OS maps
Landrangers 177 (East London) and 188 (Maidstone & Royal Tunbridge Wells), Explorers 147 (Sevenoaks & Tonbridge) and 162 (Greenwich & Gravesend)

GPS waypoints
TQ 518 615
Ⓐ TQ 512 630
Ⓑ TQ 509 639
Ⓒ TQ 506 646
Ⓓ TQ 521 654
Ⓔ TQ 523 633

This pleasant walk lies close to the M25 and is just five miles from Orpington, where suburbia ends. The outward part of the route climbs to the top of the downs and covers woodland, fields and parkland, and the return follows the lovely valley of the River Darent, passing Lullingstone Roman Villa and the World Garden of Plants at Lullingstone Castle.

Turn right out of the car park. Pass Church Street on the right; 75 yds farther on, turn left into The Landway towards Timberden Bottom. This is a steep path which strikes directly up the hill to reach a track at the edge of Meenfield Wood. Turn right and follow the track alongside the wood, with good views across Shoreham and the Darent Valley. Drop downhill, pass beside a barrier and continue ahead at a fork of paths, soon to follow the path left to a road.

Turn right then carry straight on at the road junction but 100 yds after this turn left on to Cockerhurst Road. This becomes quite steep and when it veers left leave it to the right opposite a bungalow. This footpath continues to climb beside a hawthorn thicket on the right, with fine views if you look back. Near the top of the hill bear right over a stile Ⓐ and follow a wire fence along the eastern perimeter of Dalhanna. Keep the spinney, and then a hedge, to the left as the path heads for a modern cottage near the electricity lines ahead. Bear left at the cottage to follow an enclosed path to a concrete track which leads to a lane.

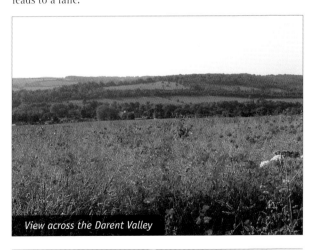

View across the Darent Valley

The hillside cross at Shoreham

Before Hulberry the path bears left. Go through the small gate **D** on your right, and follow the waymarked path around to the right. Halfway down the hill, zigzag through the hedge on your left. Here are good views of Eynsford, with its splendid red brick viaduct, as the path drops to the drive leading to Lullingstone Castle. Turn right when the path meets the drive, close to the site of Lullingstone's famous Roman villa, joining the Darent Valley Path. The river is to the left as the drive leads to the castle. The gatehouse is all that remains of the original castle – the present house is an imposing Queen Anne mansion.

This part of the route is popular with visitors to Lullingstone Park, and the path by the lake and then by the river is likely to be busy on fine days. It is a very pretty footpath which ends at the visitors' centre and **café** at the south end of the lake.

Just beyond the car park entrance, cross the stile into a field and follow the footpath parallel with the road. Continue past the 'Hop Shop' as far as the corner of the field **E**. Drop down the steps on your left, cross the road, and rejoin the Darent Valley Path as it strikes across fields to reach the riverside again. At Mill House the path turns left and then right before continuing by the River Darent to Shoreham. At the attractive old bridge turn right along Church Street and then left at the junction to return to the starting point.

Turn left here and after a short distance, at the end of the field to the right, look for steps up the bank on the right to a stile. Take the field path to pass to the left of corrugated iron sheds on the right and reach a metal gate **B** into Upper Beechen Wood. The right of way crosses straight over a footpath junction and then there is a short stretch through pleasant woodland. The path unexpectedly emerges from this on to a golf course fairway. Cross the fairway to find another small tract of woodland which gives way to a wider expanse of golf course. Follow the waymarks past the clubhouse to a Lullingstone Park noticeboard and enter the car park. Walk across to the exit gate and bear right on to the track **C**.

Pass the large green barns and modern bungalows on your right, then settle into your stride for a long stretch of straight field-edge track and path, lined with poplar trees. Cross a stile, then go through a footpath gate so the poplars are on the right.

Ancient and modern woodland around Blean

This is an excellent walk for a misty autumn day when distant views count for little. It starts in a modern wood, and moves on into tracts of woodland cared for by English Nature and known as Blean Woods, which show how woodlands were managed in previous centuries. Part of this walk may be muddy in winter.

🖊 Take the right-hand path at the top end of the car park and follow the well-surfaced forestry track, keeping ahead at a crossways. Clowes Wood has a good mix of trees, from stands of conifers to plantings of coppiced birch. After about one mile the track bends to join the course of the Canterbury and Whitstable Railway (Crab & Winkle Line) **Ⓐ**.

> **Crab and Winkle Line** This came into operation in 1830, beating the Liverpool and Manchester by a few months as the world's first steam-hauled passenger railway. It was never a success since the gradients were too severe for the locomotive (the Invicta, now preserved in Canterbury Museum) and winding engines had to be used for five miles of the six-mile route.

Soon the embankment ends and the summit is reached. There is a picnic place by a pond to the right here and a track signposted Canterbury joins from the right. Keep ahead here for 100 yds to turn right down a path at a crossing of ways **Ⓑ**. Keep ahead at a staggered crossing of paths and soon open fields can be seen to the left and right before the path reaches a farm track. Keep ahead on the track and look for a stile on the right **Ⓒ** which takes the right of way across a paddock on a slight embankment. A second stile takes the path into a field; cross the corner of this towards a house at a bend in a lane. A footbridge over a ditch takes the path to Chapel Lane. Turn right and follow it to the main road at Blean Common, cross the road and turn left, and in 75 yds take the waymarked footpath on the right which continues in the same direction along a concrete track. This ends at a covered reservoir but the path continues into Blean Woods Nature Reserve. Four woods are incorporated into the reserve, which is looked after by

walk 17

🖊 Start
Gypsy Corner, on road between Tyler Hill and Radfall

🚩 Distance
7¼ miles (11.6km)

Height gain
295 feet (90m)

🕒 Approximate time
3½ hours

Route terrain
Woodland tracks and trails and field paths

🅿 Parking
Clowes Wood Forestry Commission car park at Gypsy Corner

OS maps
Landranger 179 (Canterbury & East Kent), Explorer 150 (Canterbury & the Isle of Thanet)

GPS waypoints
🖊 TR 136 629
Ⓐ TR 125 635
Ⓑ TR 126 625
Ⓒ TR 123 617
Ⓓ TR 112 606
Ⓔ TR 107 609
Ⓕ TR 099 612
Ⓖ TR 114 620

The former Crab & Winkle line in Clowes Wood

English Nature. Continue along the track to a waymarker post and a junction of tracks at Cook's Glade. Veer right at the fork about 20 yds beyond the waymarker post **D**. Keep straight on along the left side of a clearing, and carry on again when a path leaves to the left shortly after this. Continue through the woodland until the path meets a T-junction **E**; turn left along this path, which can become very muddy.

The stile at the end of Grimshill Wood takes the footpath on to a farm track. Turn right and follow this to the road, but just before reaching it turn right on to the drive to Parsonage Farm **F**. At the farm the path continues ahead, following the bank of a ditch to a plank bridge. Once over the ditch the path resumes its easterly course and soon follows a field edge running close to a lane and crosses a last field before

meeting the lane just before a right-hand corner.

At the corner a footpath leaves the road to the left to continue a ditch-side course to the main road at Honey Hill. Turn right and pass Red Lion House and immediately after take the path left **G** beside a gate and along the edge of a field. Climb a stile at the top on to a forest track which climbs steadily, later heading in a north-easterly direction. Keep straight on when a path crosses below power lines but turn right at a T-junction to repeat a few yards of the outward route before turning left on to a track at the crossways **B**. This passes under more high voltage cables and soon the sight of picnic tables and the noise of traffic indicate that you are near the starting point, Gypsy Corner.

SCALE 1:25000 or 2½ INCHES to 1 MILE 4CM to 1KM

walk 18

Start
Cranbrook church

Distance
7¼ miles (11.6km)

Height gain
410 feet (125m)

Approximate time
3½ hours

Route terrain
Field paths and woodland tracks

P Parking
Jockey Lane car park on north side of Cranbrook church. There is another car park off High Street

OS maps
Landranger 188 (Maidstone & Royal Tunbridge Wells), Explorers 136 (High Weald, Royal Tunbridge Wells) and 137 (Ashford)

GPS waypoints
- TQ 776 362
- Ⓐ TQ 786 369
- Ⓑ TQ 793 374
- Ⓒ TQ 796 378
- Ⓓ TQ 797 384
- Ⓔ TQ 797 364
- Ⓕ TQ 798 361
- Ⓖ TQ 787 360

Cranbrook and Sissinghurst

Cranbrook was the most prosperous wool town of the Weald in medieval times and this wealth is reflected in the church with its airy space and rich glass and furniture. The footpath from the church strikes across fields and woodland to the village of Sissinghurst, famous for the gardens created by Harold Nicolson and his wife, Vita Sackville-West, around the remains of the Tudor castle. The National Trust's woodland walk reaches the castle, and the return to Cranbrook covers diverse countryside to the east of the town.

The hilltop town of Cranbrook may be justified in claiming to be the capital of the High Weald; certainly its church is known as 'the cathedral of the Weald'.

Leave the north-east corner of the churchyard, bear right to skirt the southern edge of the recreation ground and cross the road to a path on the other side. This is enclosed at first but soon emerges into open countryside.

When it approaches Great Swifts, a substantial mansion, there is a concrete section, but beyond the house, when the path swings right, leave the concrete by going ahead to a gate Ⓐ after which there is a grassy path through woodland. The path steeply descends to the next gate. Cross a meadow to a gate directly opposite, by a clump of holly bushes. Steps lead steeply down to a lane and more steps on the other side take the footpath up the bank and soon along a field edge. It crosses straight over a crossways Ⓑ and becomes a 'backway' path for a short distance before joining a drive and reaching a road.

Turn left into Sissinghurst and then right to pass the church. After the Old Vicarage turn left down a driveway. The drive ends when it reaches a sewage works but a path continues with an orchard to the left, and crosses a stream by a footbridge Ⓒ.

Almost immediately there is a kissing-gate and a sign pointing to Sissinghurst Castle. Take this path, following it through the woodland, which is carpeted with bluebells in spring, and avoid any turnings. At length you reach the main driveway.

Cross the drive, use the clapper-type stile into Park Field and follow the footpath alongside the drive, before passing through another similar stile to

Sissinghurst – the Tudor tower of the castle

SCALE 1:25000 or 2½ INCHES to 1 MILE 4CM to 1KM

rejoin it beside the old farmhouse. Keep left at a sign for the farmhouse and walk up to the visitors' car park. Turn right to visit the property, otherwise look for the waymarks indicating the route through the middle of the car park and make for a stile in the top boundary. Go diagonally right in the field towards woodland and look for a gap in the boundary. Turn left to follow a track (can be muddy), but after Horse Race House there is a surfaced drive. When this meets the road, climb the stile on the left **D** into an orchard and keep ahead following the waymarks. Follow the path round to the right in the corner of the orchard and make for its edge. Turn left here to descend to the footbridge and point **C**. From here retrace your steps to Sissinghurst village and then point **B**. Here turn left on to a path, which leads down over fields to woodland at the bottom.

In the woods cross three footbridges, then climb a steep bank to reach a stile into a meadow. Turn right and walk round the edge of the meadow to a fence and follow this to reach a stile in the corner on to a road. Turn right, climb to a junction at the top of the hill, turn right again, and walk for 100 yds before turning left **E** down a driveway, which becomes a woodland path. Continue through the woods until you see a red brick house on the left. Turn right here **F** and follow the field edge with trees and hedge on the right. Join a concrete track at the top of the field and keep ahead towards Coursehorne Farm, where surviving farm buildings have been transformed into homes. The route then follows the lane from Dulwich College Preparatory School at Coursehorne for nearly ½ mile to the road.

Turn left on to the road, and after a short distance, opposite a black and white timbered house go through the kissing-gate on the right **G** to enter a meadow. Make for an opening below, between a hedge to the left and a spinney on the right. The grassy path goes through this dip and then follows the edge of the spinney to a footbridge. Cross this and continue to walk round the edge of the woodland – there is a steep drop to a ditch. When you see the sad remains of a hedgerow, with just six or so bushes remaining, turn left to follow its line and thus reach the footpath used on the outward route, turning left to walk back to the church at Cranbrook.

Bluebell woods near Sissinghurst Castle

Penshurst and Chiddingstone

Starting at Penshurst church this walk explores the lush Eden valley, following an old track, field paths and woodland trails to the charming and timeless National Trust village of Chiddingstone, where both the church and historic Castle Inn are well worth a visit. The return route passes through the Penshurst Estate, crossing some fine parkland with good views of the mansion and the delightful surrounding countryside.

walk 19

Start
Penshurst

Distance
7½ miles (12km)

Height gain
410 feet (125m)

Approximate time
3½ hours

Route terrain
Tracks, field and woodland paths

Parking
Extended lay-by on the B2176, just north of the village opposite the long wall of Penshurst Place

OS maps
Landranger 188 (Maidstone & Royal Tunbridge Wells) and Explorer 147 (Sevenoaks & Tonbridge)

GPS waypoints
- TQ 526 437
- Ⓐ TQ 501 444
- Ⓑ TQ 503 456
- Ⓒ TQ 522 459
- Ⓓ TQ 533 459
- Ⓔ TQ 538 456
- Ⓕ TQ 535 454
- Ⓖ TQ 536 445

From the centre of the village, walk north along Penshurst Road past the **Fir Tree House Tea Rooms** on the left and Penshurst Place on the right.

> **Penshurst Place** One of the great heroes of the Elizabethan age, Sir Philip Sidney, was born in the house in 1554 and his descendants still live there. At the core of the house is the 13th-century great hall, which was built by Sir John de Poultney, four times Lord Mayor of London.

At the end of a long lay-by take the tarmac track on the left going to Salman's Farm. This is part of the Eden Valley Walk (EVW) and crosses the bridge over the River Eden. Soon after the bridge the surfaced roads swings left while the bridleway continues ahead, climbing steadily up the side of the valley and along the crest of the hill, with good views and a firm surface to make delightful walking. Another bridleway joins from the left at Wat Stock, where the track joins a tarmac lane. Pass two ponds on the right, then fork right through a gate and cross a field to reach a road beyond a gate.

Turn right for a few paces and then fork left over a stile into woodland. The EVW descends to leave the woods at a kissing-gate. In 75 yds, fork right Ⓐ at the low concrete marker to follow a path signed to 'Chiddingstone village'. Later cross a stile and turn left to climb to the top of the meadow; the pinnacles of Chiddingstone church gradually appear to the left. At the road turn left to visit the village, a showpiece street of old houses, the **Castle Inn,** a **tearoom** at Chiddingstone, and a church cared for by the National Trust. The village is often a location for films set in the 16th or 17th centuries.

To continue the walk turn right, then left immediately before the cemetery down a driveway to loop around the front garden of a house to an enclosed path, dropping down to a bridge over

Penshurst Place

the River Eden. About 30 yds beyond the bridge turn right off the path over a stile . Keep left beside the hedge, enter the next field and climb to a stile beneath trees in the top boundary. Turn right, cross a further stile in the field corner and turn left along the hedgerow, before crossing the road on to the drive towards Sandholes. Cross the stile at the end, bear left and go through a gap in the hedge, before following it eastwards to its end, where you bear left to cross a footbridge.

Beyond this, go over the field to the corner of the hedge opposite, then follow the hedge to cross a stile at the end. Continue beside the hedge, now on your left, go through a gate and cross a long meadow towards distant woods.

Chiddingstone

SCALE 1:25,000 or 2½ INCHES to 1 MILE 4CM to 1KM

Bear left through a gate, cross the ditch, then bear left on to a path above the stream to reach the road opposite Moorden **C**.

Turn right for 50 yds and turn left, passing The Barn, on to a track, which bears left then right and climbs up to a field. Follow the field-edge track ahead to a road by a railway bridge. Keep straight on along the road and turn sharp left on reaching a busier road in almost ½ mile. Cross the road and, after a few paces, turn right onto a footpath beside a row of leyland cypress trees **D**.

Pass Park Farm, bear right and descend steeply through a coppice, then climb to a broad avenue of oaks. Turn sharp right at the top **E** and walk along the avenue to a stile and gate. After 100 yds when a track comes up from the right, turn left **F** on to a field-edge track (EVW).

Pass through a spinney and continue to a gate and stile, with views on the right to Penshurst Place and its magnificent park. In 150 yds, opposite a stile to the left, turn right off the track **G** on a grassy path which heads down to a stile in the corner of the meadow. Climb this and the next stile to join the concrete driveway and turn right to follow it past Penshurst Place and church to return to Penshurst village. ●

walk 20

Linton and Boughton Monchelsea

Start	Linton church
Distance	7½ miles (12km)
Height gain	625 feet (190m)
Approximate time	3½ hours
Route terrain	Field and orchard paths, country lanes
Parking	Village car park at Linton church
OS maps	Landranger 188 (Maidstone & Royal Tunbridge Wells), Explorers 136 (High Weald, Royal Tunbridge Wells) and 148 (Maidstone & the Medway Towns)

GPS waypoints

- 📷 TQ 754 502
- Ⓐ TQ 770 500
- Ⓑ TQ 778 500
- Ⓒ TQ 777 495
- Ⓓ TQ 762 495
- Ⓔ TQ 754 494
- Ⓕ TQ 742 498
- Ⓖ TQ 734 492
- Ⓗ TQ 732 493
- Ⓙ TQ 736 505

This walk explores part of the Weald, looking down to it for some of the time from the Greensand ridge. The route is wonderful at blossom time when the orchards of the western section become a pink fairyland. In contrast the eastern section passes through the parkland of Linton and Boughton Monchelsea, where the great house is set in a deer park. The shorter version of the walk omits the western section.

📷 The start of the walk goes through the churchyard, and beyond a kissing-gate it follows the waymarked Greensand Way eastwards through parkland. It crosses the drive to Linton Park, an imposing mansion, which is seen in greater glory later. The now enclosed path runs straight and true, with parkland to the left, until it comes to the road at Loddington Oast. Cross straight over and continue to follow the path, which runs along the edge of orchards to reach Boughton Monchelsea. The Greensand Way does not go immediately to the church, which is well worth a visit for the fine views across the Weald, but swings left to join the lane farther to the north Ⓐ. Cross straight over the lane into a small chestnut grove, the path then crosses a car park and passes through parkland, with a view in winter of Boughton Monchelsea Place to the right.

After crossing the drive, the path cuts between fields towards a large oak tree in the boundary hedge. Continue ahead along the left-hand edge of a field to arrive at a crossing of paths **B**. Turn right leaving the Greensand Way and walk down the field edge, ignoring a footpath to the left just before the path drops down a steep bank. Keep close to the fence on the left, descending to a gap in the hedge on the left. Pass through it and swing right to soon locate a footbridge and kissing-gate on your right, which takes the path into Boughton Monchelsea park **C**. The fence is to the left as the path drops down to a stile where a footpath leaves to the left. Bear right here to cross the

The ancient lychgate at Boughton Monchelsea

field diagonally to reach a gate in the corner, which gives access to a lane.

Carry straight on to the next road junction and turn left to locate a stile on the right immediately after Church Farm Barn. Walk along the field edge, cross a plank bridge and stile and enter a coppice where yellow-tipped posts mark the twisting route. When the

SCALE 1:27 777 or 2⅕ INCHES to 1 MILE 3.6CM to 1KM

Boughton Monchelsea deer park

woodland ends on the left, giving way to a field, continue on the path as it descends to cross an orchard and then reach a lane **D**.

Turn left, then later, right, after gates protecting a private fishery on to a footpath that winds through scrubland to a stile leading into Linton Park. Keep the fence to the right, walking across lovely parkland with a view of the magnificent cream-coloured house whose north front was seen earlier.

Cross the iron stile close to the northern edge of the lake and then keep the railings to the left at first, soon bearing slightly to the right to reach a stile leading on to the main road.

At this point those wishing to do only the shorter version of the walk should turn right and continue along the main road to the **Bull Inn** *and Linton church.*

Turn right and then left along Wheelers Lane **E**. When the lane divides bear left into Barnes Lane and continue to the second junction where it becomes Westerhill Road. Turn left here into Bon Fleur Lane and immediately look for a stile on the right **F** to join a fenced path along the edge of a field containing an agricultural reservoir. At the end of the reservoir

bear right and continue with an orchard to the left. Cross a footbridge and follow the field edge to another orchard, where the path turns sharp left to follow its edge. Bear right at the corner of a field, following the field edge, which soon bears left beside trees to a footbridge in the corner. Cross the bridge and the field beyond, heading just to the left of a pylon on the skyline. At the field edge, keep right around Burford Farm to reach the road **G**. Turn right, then at the road junction, keep right **H** and take the waymarked footpath on the right, which runs along the side of Elm Corner Cottage. After trees the path follows the field edge and soon enters the first of a succession of orchards.

Cross over a track and turn left on to the track at the top of the orchard. Climb steeply to eventually reach the Greensand Way at the top of another orchard **J**. Turn right and follow the waymarks past the oast at Reason Hill. Cross another lane and walk through more orchards, the path eventually crossing a footbridge over a sunken lane. Walk above a spinney and cross a field before dropping down steps to the main road opposite the entrance to the car park at Linton. ●

Reculver and the Wantsum Walk

The historic remains of Reculver church are at the start of this walk and its towers are visible on the horizon for much of the way. The route follows the sea wall, then heads inland across marshes and returns on the Wantsum Walk over land which was sea in Roman times.

walk 21

Start
Reculver

Distance
8¼ miles (13.2km)

Height gain
Negligible

Approximate time
3½ hours

Route terrain
Sea wall, field paths and marshland tracks

Parking
Country park car park (Pay and Display) at Reculver

OS maps
Landranger 179 (Canterbury & East Kent), Explorer 150 (Canterbury & the Isle of Thanet)

GPS waypoints
TR 226 693
Ⓐ TR 254 676
Ⓑ TR 251 667
Ⓒ TR 237 665
Ⓓ TR 224 678

Reculver Reculver was settled by the Romans when the Isle of Thanet was truly an island and the estuary surrounding it – the Wantsum Channel – was strategically important as a sheltered haven. Reculver guarded the western entrance of the estuary, and Richborough on its eastern reach was the Roman's principal gateway into Britain. In comparison to Richborough, little of the Roman town survives at Reculver, the remains of a 3rd-century fort appearing meagre. Much more impressive are the ruins of the monastery founded by Raculf in AD669. This stands at the hub of the Roman defence works, spiritual dominance succeeding that brought by the sword. This Saxon church was enlarged in the 12th century when the twin towers, once topped with wooden spires, were added. Now all that remains are the towers – which are still valuable landmarks to mariners – some low walls and the foundations.

From the car park, where there is a tourist information centre, head eastwards (sea on the left) along the sea wall. The Roman wall and the path to the fort are to the right. The path along the sea wall passes the ruins of the abbey church on its landward side. It follows the sea wall for nearly two miles, with wide views over cropped marshes inland and equally extensive views seaward.

The sea wall swings inland to skirt a lagoon, and when it bends seaward again a path leaves to the right at a sign for the Viking Coastal Trail. Take this path to follow the bank of a reed-fringed dyke favoured by fishermen. This is easy, level walking and you will soon reach the railway crossing. Shortly after join a concrete track and head towards the church tower at St Nicholas at Wade to reach the farm and lane at Chambers Wall Ⓐ. Turn right along the lane, pass a house called Warehorn and turn right just before the busy A299. Follow the concrete road across the bridge over the dual carriageway and down the other side, before turning right along a drive.

Where the drive bears right to a house, keep straight ahead along the grassy field-edge path, passing through the edge of a spinney to reach a junction of tracks by a white cottage at Belle Isle **B**. Turn right on to Snake Drove. Do not cross the bridge on the left but keep to the concrete track to pass a pond on the right.

Just after this a dyke is crossed via a concrete bridge and then the track continues with a dyke and hedge on the left. This is Snake Drove, a concrete track with two right-angled bends. After these pass a small planting of saplings on the right and then cross the River Wantsum by another concrete bridge. The concrete track ends here, but a good track continues along the edge of the field.

At the end of the field after a concrete bridge turn right. A footbridge crossing the dyke to the left takes the footpath away over the field but the route continues on the Wantsum Walk on the eastern side of the dyke, following the waymarks. The Wantsum Walk divides at **C**, where the route bears left through double galvanised gates on to the second part of Snake Drove. The field edge track leads to a gravel track, where you turn right, then where it bends right to fishing lakes, keep ahead and follow it to the road.

Turn right along the road, beside a

The remains of Reculver church

Mud & Sand

Mussel Beds

Mud & Sand

Thanet Coastal Path

Northern Sea Wall

Knock Point

River Wantsum

6

Northern Sea Wall

Mean High

Rushbourne Sea Wall

69

Wantsum Walk

5

4

Wade Marsh

CP Bdy

3

2

3

Wade Farm

68

Pamphlet Wall

5

Bartletts

Chambers Wall

Wantsum Walk

Potten Street

ST NIC

24

25

26

A 299

Warehorn

Thanet Way

Wade House

Cemy

Wagtail

67

River Wantsum

5

5

5

Belle Isle

Pit

St Nicholas Court

St Nicholas at Wade

Sch

Wantsum Walk

Snake Drove

Wade Marsh Stream

Wantsum Walk

Saltworks

Down Barton Road

Silsoe

Down Barton

Pit (dis)

66

5

5

5

A28 Road

SCALE 1:25 000 or 2½ INCHES to 1 MILE 4CM to 1KM

| 0 | 200 | 400 | 600 | 800 METRES | 1 |
| 0 | 200 | 400 | 600 YARDS | ½ | |

KILOMETRES
MILES

dyke to the right, to eventually reach a new bridge over the Thanet Way. Cross the bridge and at the road junction which follows cross straight over to the concrete track beside a house **D**. The track heads north, descending to the railway and passing under it. After this go through a gate to walk along the right bank of a dyke, heading for Reculver towers, a pleasant end to the walk. The dyke-side path ends at a farm track where you turn left to pass a caravan site to reach the road by a **café** in Reculver. Turn right to get back to the car park.

walk 22

The Isle of Harty

Start
Leysdown-on-Sea

Distance
8 miles (12.8km)

Height gain
100 feet (30m)

Approximate time
3½ hours

Route terrain
Marshland tracks and raised flood wall

Parking
Car park on shore just to north of drive to Muswell Manor. If closed there are roadside spaces farther north towards Leysdown

OS maps
Landranger 178 (Thames Estuary), Explorer 149 (Sittingbourne & Faversham)

GPS waypoints
TR 044 697
Ⓐ TR 028 675
Ⓑ TR 024 665
Ⓒ TR 051 681

Birdwatchers will particularly appreciate this walk as will those who love wide, empty spaces with the landscape dominated by the sky. Only a dyke called the Capel Fleet separates the Isle of Harty from its mainland, the Isle of Sheppey, yet the atmosphere in this remote corner of Kent still carries the romance of the days of smugglers.

The shorter version of the walk omits remote Harty church and the Ferry Inn.

From the car park turn left along the road towards Muswell Manor. Turn right along the drive past the caravans and bear left towards the manor when a track joins the driveway from the north. When the drive bends to the left again to the house itself keep straight on. Go through a galvanised gate and pass a monument which proclaims that the first powered flight in this country by a Briton, J.T.C. Moore-Brabazon, took place near here in May 1909.

On the right are some cattlesheds. Pass these and walk

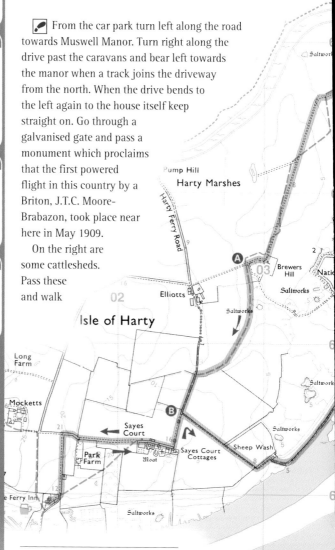

southwards on a marshland track. When it bends left, go through a pedestrian gate on the right and follow

the path. Join a track, go through a wooden kissing-gate and continue in the same direction, passing over an intersection of tracks. Keep ahead on the concrete track, the route heading farther into the Harty Marshes. From here the obvious feature is a white house, Brewers Hill, where the track bends right and skirts a clump of trees and a pond. After the last of the pollarded willow trees a track leaves to the left.

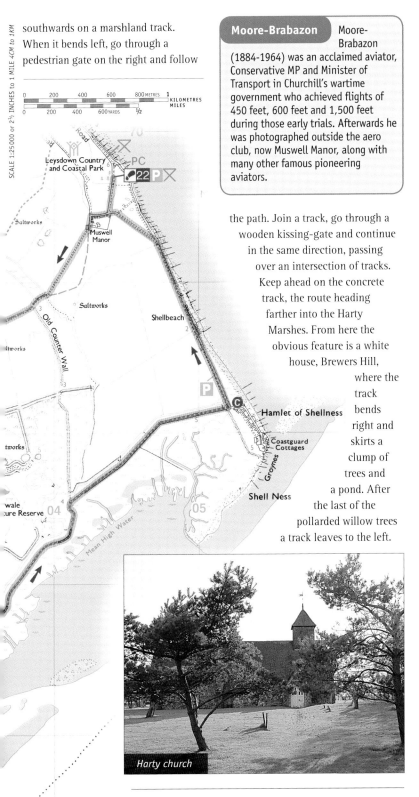

Harty church

Immediately beyond this track **Ⓐ** the right of way is to the left through an opening into the corner of a field.

Follow the left-hand edge of successive fields, eventually approaching light woodland. Look for a bridleway waymark here and follow the sometimes indistinct path ahead through scrub and trees. On reaching a track turn left and follow it to a footpath signpost **Ⓑ**.

*At this point, those who would prefer the shorter version of the walk, omitting Harty church and the Ferry Inn, should turn left and continue according to the directions after **Ⓑ** below.*

Keep ahead at the junction and turn right at the lane to reach Harty church.

Harty church

This is Kent's most remote church, dedicated to St Thomas, and is a place of great antiquity and peace. Its low walls are immensely strong and the tiled roof slopes down over these and reaches down so near to the ground on the north side that there is no space left for windows. The church originally dates from the time of the Normans though it was substantially remodelled later. It is still lit by oil lamps. Its Flemish chest dating from the 14th century with its intricate carving of a battle scene is kept in a locked side chapel, having once been stolen.

Continue along the road, passing a farmyard which was once the site of Sayes Court, the great house of Harty. Turn left at the road junction to reach **The Ferry Inn**, where an open fire is a welcome feature in winter. There is a panoramic view of the Swale, which is ¹/₂ mile wide here.

Retrace your steps to turn right at the footpath signpost **Ⓑ**, heading towards the marshy shoreline of the Swale. The landscape is empty and desolate, especially in winter. Go through a kissing-gate and swing half left to reach the sea wall. A long stretch of enjoyable walking follows along the grassy top, with a broad dyke to the left and an expanse of salt marsh on the other side. The elevated position allows views over immense distances in every direction with the huddle of houses at Shellness almost the only evidence of human settlement. Birdwatchers will constantly be using binoculars; English Nature is attempting to encourage wading birds by building earth banks in places to allow more areas to be flooded at times with shallow water.

The landscape seems unchanging; its features are so distant that the approach to them is imperceptible at first. Getting closer, the details of the houses at Shellness can be seen. This is a private hamlet and when the path reaches the lane **Ⓒ** there is no choice except to turn left along the top of the bank.

It is soon possible to cross to the beach itself but note that there is a naturists' beach here, just before the next little unnamed settlement of bungalows. Keep straight ahead to return to the starting point. ●

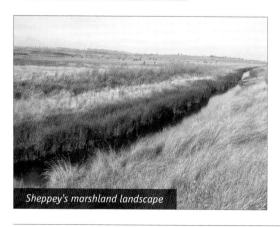

Sheppey's marshland landscape

Oare Creek and The Swale

Hollingbourne and Thurnham

This route offers a fine physical challenge as well as the opportunity of enjoying one of the best sections of the North Downs Way, with the path constantly dipping and climbing. The views from the top of the ridge must be among the finest to be had from the North Downs Way.

Start
Hollingbourne

Distance
7½ miles (12km)

Height gain
1,115 feet (340m)

Approximate time
4 hours

Route terrain
Field paths, downland trails and country lanes

P Parking
Limited spaces in the main street at Hollingbourne, in the vicinity of the Dirty Habit pub. If visiting the inn you can use the car park (please advise staff)

OS maps
Landranger 188 (Maidstone & Royal Tunbridge Wells), Explorer 148 (Maidstone & the Medway Towns)

GPS waypoints
- TQ 844 553
- Ⓐ TQ 826 562
- Ⓑ TQ 821 569
- Ⓒ TQ 808 580
- Ⓓ TQ 825 576
- Ⓔ TQ 841 566

From the **Dirty Habit** pub take the lane opposite for Thurnham, an easy start to the walk along a quiet narrow road, with the downs rising in an arc to the right. On reaching the hamlet of Broad Street, turn left after the Old House down a driveway, with an oast house to the right. The drive gives way to an enclosed path that ends when it reaches an open field. The right of way runs across farmland heading in a south-westerly direction.

Make for the left-hand corner of the woodland to the right Ⓐ, and you will come to a lone tree where five footpaths meet. A waymarker post stands by the tree. Turn sharp right and then follow the path with the wood to the left before walking beside a ditch to reach the drive leading to Ripple Manor. Turn right on to the drive that winds down to a cottage Ⓑ. Just before the cottage, at the beginning of a row of leylandii, turn left along an enclosed path that skirts the garden and cross two stiles to reach a paddock. Keep ahead with fences to the left, crossing several stiles, to reach steps that take you down towards Cobham Manor Riding Centre.

From the car park, where there is a **coffee shop**, head for the lane and turn left. Directly opposite the manor take a path

Downland landscape near Hollingbourne

on the right which heads along the field edge towards an oast house, where it meets a gate and a surfaced bridleway.

Continue along this to reach Thurnham Lane and turn right to climb the hill, passing the **Black Horse**, at the crossroads.

Keep straight on at the intersection and climb the steep hill to reach a hairpin bend where the North Downs Way leaves to the right **C**. Take this path below the overgrown ramparts of Thurnham Castle, with a steep combe away to your right.

The Dirty Habit pub in Hollingbourne

Turn right through a gate at the top of the combe to skirt the top of the field, following the fence on the right to a gate before descending steps below Civiley Wood. After these there is a much longer flight of steps to climb to reach the crest of the downs once again. Some glorious walking follows along a roller coaster of a path with a fine view to the right. More steps, up and down, follow through yew trees and fallen beeches.

The path eventually drops down to cross Coldblow Lane and a steep climb follows to the crest of the downs again near Cat's Mount. The North Downs Way now becomes a fenced field-edge path with wide views to the south. It then descends steps again to cross the neck of a large field to meet a byway **D**. This is Coldharbour Lane; turn left and follow it up to reach the top of the ridge once again. Here the North Downs Way leaves to the right. Follow it as it wends its way through woodland just below the crest of the downs as before.

The path emerges from woodland and then crosses a large field. After this it crosses another field above Broad Street, soon to follow the boundary close by on the right to reach a stile and another road. Cross over to resume walking along the ridge on a grassy path. A further flight of steps in a wood takes the path down to the byway **E** that climbs up from Allington Farm. Turn left for a short way up this muddy track and then turn off right on to a winding path that passes through Hucking Estate woodland.

For a short distance the path meanders through the trees and then the woodland suddenly ends and a wide view over the Weald is revealed. Another short stretch of woodland follows before the path reaches open hillside again. Continue to follow North Downs Way signs, bearing right towards Hollingbourne when you reach a lone waymarker post on the downland slope and the church and village can be seen below. The path does not join the road immediately, however, but runs parallel to and above it. It then descends gradually to meet the road just north of the village. ●

St Margaret's Bay and The South Foreland

walk 24

Start
St Margaret's at Cliffe

Distance
8¼ miles (13.2km),
including an optional
4-mile (6.5km) return
spur along the Saxon
Shore Way & White
Cliffs Country Trail to
the National Trust
visitor centre at
Langdon Cliff

Height gain
1,065 feet (325m)

Approximate time
4 hours

Route terrain
Downland tracks and
cliff paths

Parking
Car park near the
church in the centre of
St Margaret's at Cliffe

OS maps
Landranger 179
(Canterbury & East
Kent), Explorer 138
(Dover, Folkestone &
Hythe)

GPS waypoints
TR 358 447
Ⓐ TR 361 452
Ⓑ TR 367 459
Ⓒ TR 367 440
Ⓓ TR 359 433
Ⓔ TR 334 421

This is a spectacular walk in any season but particularly on a bright, sunny day when the French coast is visible just 20 miles across the Channel. From the inland village of St Margaret's at Cliffe the route is across open country to the renowned White Cliffs of Dover, an iconic and much-loved British landmark. Climb up to the South Foreland Lighthouse where there is an optional spur to Langdon Cliff, which offers uninterrupted views of Dover harbour and its bustling activity.

Walk to the car park entrance on the High Street and turn left. Pass the parish church, then right at the **Red Lion** into Kingsdown Road. At the end of a line of houses Ⓐ keep ahead on the signposted cycle trail. Avoid a path on the left, pass the entrance to Little Banks on the right and keep right at the fork to join a path Ⓑ. Cross a stile and pass a National Trust sign for Bockhill Farm. Follow the path as it curves right, cutting between fields with the horizon defined by the English Channel and a distinctive obelisk. Merge with a track and as it veers right to approach farm outbuildings, maintain the same direction by following a field path running to the left of a hedge.

On reaching a junction with the Saxon Shore Way & White Cliffs Country Trail, turn right towards the **Bluebirds Tearoom** and the Dover Patrol Memorial, which was designed by Sir Aston Webb and is one of three constructed by public subscription in memory of almost 2,000 men in the Dover Patrol lost during the First World War. Pass the memorial and Bluebirds Tearoom and then turn left at a National Trust sign for The Leas. Follow the grassy path down between the English Channel and the road. South Foreland Lighthouse can be seen on the horizon. Gradually St Margaret's Bay edges into view. Pass a seat and a viewing point and when the path divides keep left and follow it through some trees, down to a kissing-gate. Turn left at a flight of steps and follow them down to the bay.

During the 1950s James Bond author, Ian Fleming, lived at the striking Art Deco house on the beach at the northern end of St Margaret's Bay. The house was previously owned by Noel Coward. Fleming set his 007 novel *Moonraker* on this stretch of

St Margaret's Bay

coast, using the spectacular setting to great effect. Walk along the seafront to the **Coastguard** public house and then head uphill by road, following the sign for the Saxon Shore Way. At the hairpin, leave the road and keep straight on for a few paces, then left into Beach Road. Pass between the organically managed Pines Garden and a **tearoom** and continue uphill to a cattle-grid and gate.

Take the steps to the left of them, go through a kissing-gate and up the grassy slope to merge with a track **C**. Walk towards South Foreland Lighthouse, pass a gate and cattle-grid and a National Trust sign for Lighthouse Down before passing a windmill half hidden by trees. On reaching a junction turn left by a cattle-grid towards the lighthouse and the main entrance. Completed in 1843, the South Foreland Lighthouse is owned by the National Trust and open to visitors at certain times of the year. The main walk turns right at this point to join a waymarked footpath **D**.

To reach the visitor centre at

Langdon Cliff take the path along the beacon's seaward side and here the clifftop path resumes its south-westerly course towards Dover. Follow the spectacular Saxon Shore Way and White Cliffs Country Trail for about 2 miles, making for the National Trust visitor centre and **café E**. *From here retrace your steps and take the waymarked path at* **D**.

Pass between fields and woodland and on reaching a junction with a track, turn right. Follow it to the edge of St Margaret's at Cliffe and turn left at path ER33 just before a row of bungalows. Follow the path through the trees and then diagonally across a field towards houses. Cut through a tunnel of trees to the road and turn right through a housing estate. Take the first left turning (Reach Close) and then right at Reach Road. At the junction with the High Street, turn left and return to the car park. ●

SCALE 1:25000 or 2½ INCHES to 1 MILE 4CM to 1KM

walk 25

Wye and Crundale Downs

Start
Wye church

Distance
8½ miles (13.5km)

Height gain
1,050 feet (320m)

Approximate time
4 hours

Route terrain
Field paths, woodland trails and downland byways

Parking
Small car park signed off Churchfield Way just west of the church, or roadside on Churchfield Way in front of the green

OS maps
Landranger 179 (Canterbury & East Kent) or 189 (Ashford & Romney Marsh), Explorer 137 (Ashford)

GPS waypoints
TR 054 468
Ⓐ TR 062 469
Ⓑ TR 067 473
Ⓒ TR 074 477
Ⓓ TR 076 488
Ⓔ TR 084 485
Ⓕ TR 087 468
Ⓖ TR 082 462
Ⓗ TR 086 448
Ⓙ TR 077 457
Ⓚ TR 070 469

A section of this walk which uses the North Downs Way has some spectacular long-distance views. Elsewhere on the route there are many other, more intimate views of the Kent countryside, which give just as much pleasure. The outward leg uses part of the Stour Valley Walk and the long section which follows heading south is on a quiet byway and footpath along the crest of the Crundale Downs.

Walk along Churchfield Way towards the church. Follow the Stour Valley Walk waymark through the churchyard to the north-east corner, on to a footpath which passes allotments and bears right past the former Wye Agricultural College buildings to cross a road on to Occupation Road, which is waymarked with a North Downs Way logo.

Pass sheds and nurseries, the road becoming a track sheltered by conifers and poplars as it heads towards the escarpment of the downs. Leave the track by turning left on a path Ⓐ across fields, following the Stour Valley Walk emblem. After a spinney, cross a road to a track, which leads up through trees to a radio mast. Bear off left before the mast to follow a path through beech trees and then cross another lane. Exit the trees Ⓑ and turn right on to a good field track. At the end of the wood follow a path left across the field, rising steeply as it nears

View from Crundale Downs

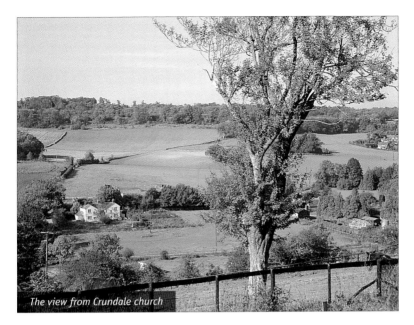
The view from Crundale church

narrow Beech Wood on the far side.

Climb through the wood and up to the top of the meadow beyond. The path dips down into a hollow, then rises to cross a stile beside a gate to reach a junction of five ways on the edge of Warren Wood **C**. Turn left along the Stour Valley Walk, the path following the edge of Warren Wood with a fence to the right before heading deeper into the wood. Keep to the main path, which soon becomes a grassy track as it descends steeply to leave the wood. Turn immediately left off the track to follow a path north across a downland meadow below the wood to meet a track **D** at the far end of the wood.

Turn right and walk past the northern end of Marriage Wood on a lovely green lane. Descend to the second white house, pass to the right of it and follow the track as it climbs up the flank of the hill, but before the top turn right on to another bridleway and then almost immediately left over a stile by a gate to the left **E**. Climb to the top of the paddock to a stile opposite the east end of Crundale's early Norman church and

turn right on to a good track, which strikes south along the top of the Crundale Downs.

This is exhilarating walking, with larks singing above and ever-changing views over an expanse of countryside. Almost too soon you come to Towns Wood, where the track through it may become muddy in winter. The track eventually drops down to meet and cross a lane **F** leading to Hassell Street. Follow a path along the right-hand edge of two fields on a generous headland to reach a gate. Descend into the crater to find a stile on the other side, then follow the grassy track to the bottom of the field **G** and turn left to follow the fence away from Coombe Manor.

The path climbs up to the woods again to a stile at the end of the field. Go through the gate ahead and keep to the right-hand side of a paddock to a stile. Cross the next two fields diagonally to a stile at the top corner. The stile after this takes the path on to the drive from Stoackes Cottage. Turn left and follow it to the road at Folly Town.

Cross the road and walk past Staple Farm and the farmyard at Cold Blow. Turn right through a gate, before the National Nature Reserve's noticeboard, on to the North Downs Way **H**. The path goes across the field to a field-edge path, which skirts the top of Newgate Scrubs to reach open downland, where you have glorious views across the Wealden countryside. Rare plants, including orchids like the Maid of Kent or lady orchid, are found here. The road is close to the right and to the left is the Devil's Kneading Trough, a spectacular steep-sided combe. After leaving the reserve the North Downs Way crosses the road to a byway **J**.

Almost immediately, turn left through a gate, following the North Downs Way alongside the fence to the right, with Wye coming into view ahead. Continue over the high ground, passing a viewpoint to reach a stile. The path skirts round the top of a small piece of woodland to reach a lane. Turn left, then leave the road to the left **K** just before it swings right, following the North Downs Way on to a bridleway through a wood, then along the edge of a field and across a road before rejoining the outward route at **A**. ●

SCALE 1:25000 or 2½ INCHES to 1 MILE 4CM to 1KM

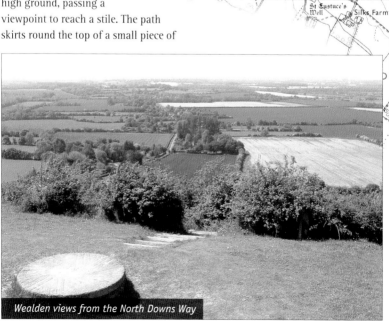

Wealden views from the North Downs Way

Bridge, Bishopsbourne and Pett Bottom

Start
Bridge

Distance
9½ miles (15.2km)

Height gain
805 feet (245m)

Approximate time
4½ hours

Route terrain
Field paths, woodland trails, quiet country lanes

Parking
Bridge – at recreation ground, Patrixbourne Road, or on-street

OS maps
Landranger 179 (Canterbury & East Kent) or 189 (Ashford & Romney Marsh), Explorers 150 (Canterbury & the Isle of Thanet) and 138 (Dover, Folkestone & Hythe)

GPS waypoints
📍 TR 183 541
Ⓐ TR 184 533
Ⓑ TR 196 499
Ⓒ TR 186 506
Ⓓ TR 166 509
Ⓔ TR 163 531
Ⓕ TR 169 524

The ancient city of Canterbury is surrounded by an undulating countryside of orchards, parkland and woodland. This walk has all of these and visits two attractive villages en route, as well as a remote country pub at the charmingly named Pett Bottom.

Bridge Sir Nikolaus Pevsner, in *The Buildings of England*, is very unkind to Bridge, calling it 'a dour main-road village' with a church which was restored in 1859–60 'with grotesque insensitivity'. However justified the latter comment, the first is unfair and inaccurate today as Bridge has been bypassed and is now a pleasant and peaceful backwater away from the noisy bustle of the Dover Road.

Start with the church on your right and walk forward to take Bourne Park Road, which leaves the main road to the right. Go through the gate on the left in 50 yds into Bourne Park on the Elham Valley Way. Keep the lane close to the right as you walk towards the left-hand edge of the spinney ahead and on reaching it follow the fence to a gate leading into Warren Plantation. A short woodland path leads to a lane, where you turn left to pass the drive to Bourne House.

Go through the gate on the right, almost opposite the end of the lake Ⓐ and head for Bishopsbourne church in the distance ahead. There is an excellent view of Bourne House from here – a beautiful early 18th-century mansion in a fine setting. Go through a gate and cross two footbridges to enter the churchyard by a gate on the left. The house to the left of the church, Oswalds, was the last home of the novelist Joseph Conrad, who lived there for five years until his death in 1924.

Take the Kingston road from the church, pass **The Mermaid** pub, and when the road swings left keep straight on along the bridleway into Charlton Park. When the drive swings right take the bridleway left through a metal gate and follow the right-hand field edge, soon to cross a little brick bridge. Go through several gates, following an enclosed path into Kingston, turning left at the road and then right up Church Lane. Pass the

The Nail Bourne at Bishopsbourne

church lychgate to reach two footpaths, one each side of a house called Littlecourt. Take the left path into a paddock and bear diagonally right to cross two paddocks to reach a road by a railway bridge.

Go under the bridge and follow the road to a bridleway on the left, just beyond a pumping station. Walk through woodland then climb gently towards two houses, one of them called Heart's Delight. Keep right at the fork to pass in front of the house **B**, then head right at the next fork to climb to a gate to enter Knowle Wood. Descend through the trees to a gate, then keep the wood and then a hedge to the right and descend to a gate and road at the bottom of the meadow. Turn right along the road for a few paces and then turn

left to walk up an enclosed bridleway, climbing the opposite side of the valley to another lane. Turn right and then left after The Hermitage to continue following the bridleway uphill. After a gate keep the fence to the right to meet a third lane. Turn left, then at the top of the hill **C** turn right along a track (can be muddy) into Charlton Wood.

When the track bears right, follow the waymark left, keep right when the path forks and then pass between tall leylandi trees to reach a field edge path with the wood to the right. At the end of the trees turn right then immediately left to cross a footpath. The track crosses between fields, heading for more trees, and then swings left and descends to the road at Langham Park Barn. Turn right then left at the junction

Bishopsbourne

and climb beside woodland towards Bursted Manor. Reach the top of the hill and then descend steeply, passing a track to Whitebeams on the left, to turn right in 100 yds over a stile **D**. Follow the top edge of the field, cross two drives, the path becoming narrow and enclosed below Gorsley House.

Pass a large shed, the path then follows the edge of a wood with views over paddocks and fields. If necessary there is a path on the left through trees and across a field to **The Duck** pub at Pett Bottom. Exit the wood and continue in the same direction across a large field, passing close to a pylon, to reach the road. Turn right, pass Little Eaton Farm and continue for ¼ mile to a footpath and stile on the right **E**. Follow the left-hand field edge to a stile and carry on in the same direction, bearing right at the field boundary to cross a stile on the left. Follow the left-hand hedge, looking down to the farm and cottages at Little Pett.

Go through the gap in the hedge at the end of the field and head half-right to the corner of woods at the top of the rise. Keep the woodland to the right and turn left across the field at a waymark **F** to reach a stile. Cross the stile and continue ahead, following the path along the edge of fields and orchards to

a stile. Beyond, a field edge path leads to a gate, where you cross the old railway line to join a track, with Bridge visible ahead. In a few paces take the path right across the field and drop down the left-hand edge of the next

SCALE 1:25000 or 2½ INCHES to 1 MILE 4CM to 1KM

field towards a fine brick mansion.
Cross a stile and bear left across
meadows to cross two footbridges over
the Nail Bourne stream to reach a gate
and lane. Turn right and follow the lane
left back into Bridge.

walk 27

Oare Marshes, the Swale and Luddenham

Start
Oare

Distance
10 miles (16km)

Height gain
165 feet (50m)

Approximate time
4½ hours

Route terrain
Grassy sea wall, field and orchard paths, quiet country lanes

Parking
Roadside spaces by the Castle Inn and along Church Road. Alternatively, use free car park at Oare Marshes Nature Reserve (Point **A**)

OS maps
Landranger 178 (Thames Estuary), Explorer 149 (Sittingbourne & Faversham)

GPS waypoints
TR 007 628
A TR 013 647
B TQ 966 654
C TQ 962 645
D TQ 972 629
E TQ 990 626
F TQ 998 631

The landscape of the marshes facing the Swale may appear desolate to some, but others will love the empty horizons as they tread the springy turf on top of the Swaleside flood wall. Birdwatchers should take their binoculars, especially in winter to view waders, duck and geese on Oare Marshes Nature Reserve. The return walk to Oare follows field paths and quiet lanes to the lost village of Luddenham.

Walk to the **Castle Inn** at the head of Oare Creek and enter the track on the left, passing through a kissing-gate on the right to join a path leading to another gate at the side of a boatyard. After a brief enclosed section the route follows the side of Oare Creek on a grassy path on top of the flood bank. This is part of the Saxon Shore Way, which follows the coast of Kent and Sussex from Gravesend to Rye – a distance of 140 miles. To the left is Oare church, atop the only hill in the vicinity. Moorings and boatyards line the opposite bank of the creek and the Shipwrights Arms, at Hollowshore, marks the end of these boatyards.

When the path goes beneath the electricity cables, Harty church on the Isle of Sheppey can be seen ahead, also on a slight hill. The path enters the Oare Marshes Nature Reserve, set up to protect this area of traditional north Kent grazing marsh by keeping water levels high enough to encourage wading birds.

Oare Creek

Boatyard at Oare

The view changes as the path turns westwards at the mouth of the creek, where ribs of long abandoned vessels lie on the mudflats. The path reaches the slipway once used by the Harty Ferry, where there is information about the nature reserve, and a car park **Ⓐ**. A galvanised gate by an abandoned jetty marks the end of the reserve and after this you continue west along the top of the bank. This is a wonderfully lonely part of the walk, with glorious marsh and estuary views, and in the distance the bascules of the Kingsferry Bridge can be seen.

In the estuary is a small island appropriately named Fowley Island and towards the end of this the path swings away from the Swale **Ⓑ**, passing a gate on the right. Head inland to a gate, where the embankment ends and soon enter a thicket before emerging on to a common-like area, the site of a former gunpowder factory, one of four explosives factories on the Uplees

Marshes during the First World War.

The path leads past modern timber-built houses on the right before reaching Conyer where **The Ship** stands by the creek. Walk up the main street, past houses on the left and houseboats in the creek on the right, to where the road bends left **Ⓒ**.

Follow the road round to the left and opposite Brunswick House take a footpath on the right to cut a corner, walking behind houses and across a paddock to a gate and road. Continue along the road and keep straight on at the road junction at Banks Farm, along Teynham Street, and at Peete House where a path cuts another corner by following a line of poplars.

Rejoin and carry on along the road and immediately before the houses at Deerton Street **Ⓓ** take a footpath to the left, which leads beside an orchard and across a field. Keep the conifer windbreaks to the left and cross a track leading to the Old Farmhouse to reach a lane; turn left. The lane soon bends sharply right; there are views over the marshes. Continue, soon climbing steadily, until just after the crest there is a gate on the left by a lone poplar **E**. Go through the gate on to a path to Luddenham, a forgotten village

comprising a fine house, outbuildings around a farmyard, and a small, disused church.

Turn right out of the farmyard at the end of a barn and cross two fields to reach a lane. Cross straight over to join a track, then where it bends left **F**

leave it at a marker post and head across the field, making for telegraph poles. Pass close to the lower pole and walk across the field to a gate in its lower right corner. *(If this field is impassable, there is an easy alternative from* **F** *: keep on the track and turn right on to the road.)* From the field gate, turn right and soon walk down the main street of Oare to the **Three Mariners** pub and Church Road.

SCALE 1:25 000 or 2½ INCHES to 1 MILE 4CM to 1KM

walk 28

Start
The Square, Chilham

Distance
10¼ miles (16.4km)

Height gain
1,065 feet (325m)

Approximate time
5 hours

Route terrain
Field paths, woodland and parkland bridleways, quiet country lanes

Parking
Car park at western entrance to Chilham off A252

OS maps
Landrangers 179 (Canterbury & East Kent) or 189 (Ashford & Romney Marsh), Explorers 137 (Ashford) or 149 (Sittingbourne & Faversham)

GPS waypoints
TR 068 535
Ⓐ TR 055 520
Ⓑ TR 074 507
Ⓒ TR 081 510
Ⓓ TR 089 515
Ⓔ TR 085 520
Ⓕ TR 089 519
Ⓖ TR 090 532
Ⓗ TR 092 538
Ⓙ TR 080 531
Ⓚ TR 071 525

Chilham, Godmersham and the Stour Valley

Chilham is one of Kent's showpiece villages with its church and castle on opposite sides of a lovely square lined with ancient houses – an arrangement which reflects the feudal nature of the medieval village. The walk covers diverse countryside around the village, using parts of the Stour Valley Walk and the North Downs Way as well as lesser-used bridleways and footpaths.

> **Chilham** Chilham Castle is a red brick Jacobean mansion which replaced an octagonal 12th-century stronghold, the remains of which can still be seen. The village church, St Mary's, has exceptional monuments and original glass.

From the gateway to the castle at the top end of the Square, walk down School Hill with the outer castle walls to the right. At the road junction keep straight on to join Mountain Street, the brick wall blocking off views of the castle until opposite the lake where it gives way briefly to railings through which there is a vista to the great house in its setting. The lake is the site of an 800-year-old heronry.

Continue along Mountain Street, then at the hilltop, where the lane bends sharp left, carry straight on, following the North Downs Way. Keep to the track when it turns right and begins to climb steadily. At the top, with woods to the right, leave the North Downs Way before the Kings Wood signboard by turning left over a stile Ⓐ by Godmersham Park Deer Leap. After crossing the field the path comes to a meadow where it continues downhill, heading towards the right-hand end of a wood to join a track into Godmersham Park.

There is an ever-improving view of the house as the track descends into the valley past a succession of paddocks.

> **Godmersham Park House** The red brick house dates from 1732 and was once owned by Edward Knight, Jane Austen's brother. She frequently visited him and it provided her with details, which she used in *Mansfield Park* and *Pride and Prejudice*.

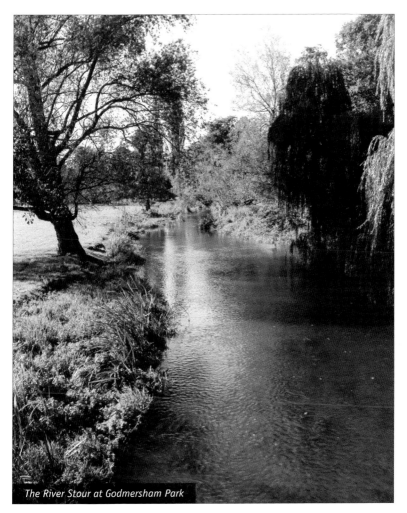
The River Stour at Godmersham Park

Keep straight on across a drive and pass yet more paddocks to reach the meadow before the river. Turn right and follow the yellow arrow on an oak tree to reach the driveway by the lodge. Turn left, cross the bridge over the River Stour and walk up to the main road; cross this too into The Street. Go under the railway and turn left down Eggarton Lane. The lane bends right away from the railway then shortly beyond Home Farm, at the end of a spinney on the left **B**, follow the Stour Valley Way left and cross the field diagonally.

Keep ahead over the next field towards the left-hand end of the line of trees at the top **C**. There is a grand view from here. The path goes left around the wood, then through the trees and soon crosses a stile before descending diagonally across a meadow to a stile and lane opposite Woodsdale Farm.

Turn right, pass Forest Farmhouse, and soon after this, when the track swings right, climb the stile on the left and cross the paddock – you are now on the Stour Valley Walk. Turn left up the field edge in the next field to a stile and enter a wood. Walk through this short piece of woodland, still climbing, to reach a footpath junction **D**. Turn left,

View across the Stour Valley

emerge from the trees, then cross a farm track and follow the field edge down to Down Wood. This is atmospheric woodland and the path goes through tunnels of yew bushes before reaching a footpath junction **E**. Turn sharp right and leave the Stour Valley Way.

The path is narrow and steep and from the fence at the top of the wood walk ahead to meet a signposted track. Swing left at the wooden post **F** to walk northwards over cultivated land with the wood close to the right.

Enter the woodland, gently descend on the bridleway and, just before reaching open country, swing off the track to the left, this pleasant detour meandering through the trees, with a field away to the right. Look for a turning on the right, leading to the edge of the woodland **G**. Take the path and cross the field to the end of the hedgerow directly in front where there is a pit. Then follow the hedge, and later a fence, to join Pig Lane.

Pass Mystole Farm on the right to reach a surfaced drive and turn left to meet a lane at a sharp bend **H**. Turn left here on to a byway, which gives good views of the Stour Valley lakes, originally gravel workings and now a fishery. When the track climbs out of trees, low hedges allow more views of

the valley and of Chilham. Keep ahead when a footpath leaves to the right **J** that descends to Chilham Mill and can be used as a short cut back to the village. Continue along the track (can be muddy) until the Stour Valley Path leaves to the left at a crossways. Take the track ahead, which descends to East Stour Farm; the scenery here is particularly delightful.

At the end of the track cross a stile

and turn right to pass under the railway and reach the main road. Turn left along the verge for 100 yds and then cross it to a footbridge over the river. Make your way across two fields towards Chilham Castle, which can be seen in the distance, and after about ¼ mile look for a stile in the left boundary

. Cross this, heading diagonally right across the field to locate a path leading to the road at Mountain Street, at which point you turn right to retrace your steps to Chilham.

Further Information

 Walking Safety

Although the reasonably gentle countryside that is the subject of this book offers no real dangers to walkers at any time of the year, it is still advisable to take sensible precautions and follow certain well-tried guidelines.

Always take with you both warm and waterproof clothing and sufficient food and drink. Wear suitable footwear, such as strong walking boots or shoes that give a good grip over stony ground, on slippery slopes and in muddy conditions. Try to obtain a local weather forecast and bear it in mind before you start. Do not be afraid to abandon your proposed route and return to your starting point in the event of a sudden and unexpected deterioration in the weather.

All the walks described in this book will be safe to do, given due care and respect, even during the winter. Indeed, a crisp, fine winter day often provides perfect walking conditions, with firm ground underfoot and a clarity unique to this time of the year. The most difficult hazard likely to be encountered is mud, especially when walking along woodland and field paths, farm tracks and bridleways – the latter in particular can often get churned up by cyclists and horses. In summer, an additional difficulty may be narrow and overgrown paths, particularly along the edges of cultivated fields. Always ensure appropriate footwear is worn.

 Walkers and the Law

The Countryside and Rights of Way Act (CRoW Act 2000) extends the rights of access previously enjoyed by walkers in England and Wales. Implementation of these rights began on 19 September 2004. The Act amends existing legislation and for the first time provides access on foot to certain types of land – defined as mountain, moor, heath, down and registered common land.

Where You Can Go
Rights of Way
Prior to the introduction of the CRoW Act, walkers could only legally access the countryside along public rights of way. These are either 'footpaths' (for walkers only) or 'bridleways' (for walkers, riders on horseback and pedal cyclists). A third category called 'Byways open to all traffic' (BOATs), is used by motorised vehicles as well as those using non-mechanised transport. Mainly they are green lanes, farm and estate roads, although occasionally they will be found crossing mountainous area.

Rights of way are marked on Ordnance Survey maps. Look for the green broken lines on the Explorer maps, or the red dashed lines on Landranger maps.

The term 'right of way' means exactly what it says. It gives a right of passage over what, for the most part, is private land. Under pre-CRoW legislation walkers were required to keep to the line of the right of way and not stray onto land on either side. If you did inadvertently wander off the right of way, either because of faulty map reading or because the route was not clearly indicated on the ground, you were technically trespassing.

Local authorities have a legal obligation to ensure that rights of way are kept clear and free of obstruction, and are signposted where they leave metalled roads. The duty of local authorities to install signposts extends to the placing of signs along a path or way, but only where the authority considers it necessary to have a signpost or waymark to assist persons unfamiliar with the locality.

The New Access Rights
Access Land
As well as being able to walk on existing rights of way, under the new legislation you now have access to large areas of open land. You can of course continue to use rights of way footpaths to cross this land, but the main difference is that you can now

lawfully leave the path and wander at will, but only in areas designated as access land.

Where to Walk

Areas now covered by the new access rights – Access Land – are shown on Ordnance Survey Explorer maps bearing the access land symbol on the front cover.

'Access Land' is shown on Ordnance Survey maps by a light yellow tint surrounded by a pale orange border. New orange coloured 'i' symbols on the maps will show the location of permanent access information boards installed by the access authorities.

Restrictions

The right to walk on access land may lawfully be restricted by landowners, but whatever restrictions are put into place on access land they have no effect on existing rights of way, and you can continue to walk on them.

Dogs

Dogs can be taken on access land, but must be kept on leads of two metres or less between 1 March and 31 July, and at all times where they are near livestock. In addition land-owners may impose a ban on all dogs from fields where lambing takes place for up to six weeks in any year. Dogs may be banned from moorland used for grouse shooting and breeding for up to five years.

General Obstructions

Obstructions can sometimes cause a problem on a walk and the most common of these is where the path across a field has been ploughed over. It is legal for a farmer to plough up a path provided that it is restored within two weeks. This does not always happen and you are faced with the dilemma of following the line of the path, even if this means treading on crops, or walking round the edge of the field. Although the latter course of action seems the most sensible, it does mean that you would be trespassing.

Other obstructions can vary from overhanging vegetation to wire fences across the path, locked gates or even a cattle feeder on the path.

Use common sense. If you can get round the obstruction without causing damage, do so. Otherwise only remove as much of the obstruction as is necessary to secure passage.

If the right of way is blocked and cannot be followed, there is a long-standing view that in such circumstances there is a right to deviate, but this cannot wholly be relied on. Although it is accepted in law that highways (and that includes rights of way) are for the public service, and if the usual track is impassable, it is for the general good that people should be entitled to pass into another line. However, this should not be taken as indicating a right to deviate when-ever a way is impassable. If in doubt, retreat.

Report obstructions to the local authority and/or the Ramblers.

 Useful Organisations

Campaign to Protect Rural England
128 Southwark St, London SE1 0SW
Tel. 020 7981 2800
www.cpre.org.uk

English Heritage
Kemble Drive, Swindon SN2 2YP
Tel. 01793 414700
www.english-heritage.org.uk

National Trust
Membership and General Enquiries
PO Box 39, Warrington WA5 7WD
Tel. 0844 800 1895
www.nationaltrust.org.uk

Natural England
33rd Floor, Touthill Close, City Road,
Peterborough PE1 1XN
Tel. 0845 600 3078
www.naturalengland.org.uk

Ordnance Survey
Tel. 08456 050505
www.ordnancesurvey.co.uk

The Ramblers
2nd Floor, Camelford House
87-90 Albert Embankment, London
SE1 7TW
Tel. 020 7339 8500
www.ramblers.org.uk

Youth Hostels Association
Trevelyan House, Dimple Road
Matlock, Derbyshire DE4 3YH
Tel. 01629 592600
www.yha.org.uk

Traveline
0871 200 2233

National Train Enquiry Line
08457 484950

Tourist Information Centres
Ashford: 01233 629165
Canterbury: 01227 378100
Deal: 01304 369576
Dover: 01304 205108

Faversham: 01795 534542
Maidstone: 01622 602169
Margate: 01843 577577
Rochester: 01634 843666
Sandwich: 01304 613565
Sevenoaks: 01732 450305
Tenterden: 01233 330316
Tonbridge: 01732 770929
Tunbridge Wells: 01892 515675

Kent County Council
County Hall, Maidstone Kent ME14 1XQ
0845 8247905
www.kent.gov.uk

 Ordnance Survey maps for Kent

Kent is covered by Ordnance Survey 1:50 000 scale (1$\frac{1}{4}$ inches to 1 mile or 2cm to 1km) Landranger map sheets 177, 178, 179, 187, 188 and 189. These all-purpose maps are packed with information to help you explore the area. Viewpoints, picnic sites, places of interest, and caravan and camping sites are shown, as well as public rights of way information such as footpaths and bridleways.

To examine Kent in more detail, and especially if you are planning walks, Ordnance Survey Explorer maps at 1:25 000 scale (2$\frac{1}{2}$ inches to 1 mile or 4cm to 1km) are ideal:

125 (Romney Marsh, Rye & Winchelsea)
136 (High Weald, Royal Tunbridge Wells)
137 (Ashford)
138 (Dover, Folkestone & Hythe)
147 (Sevenoaks & Tonbridge)
148 (Maidstone & the Medway Towns)
149 (Sittingbourne & Faversham)
150 (Canterbury & the Isle of Thanet)
163 (Gravesend & Rochester)

Text:	John Brooks and Tony Durrant
	Revised text for 2005 edition, Nick Channer and David Foster,
	2007 edition Nick Channer, 2014 edition David Hancock
Photography:	David Hancock, John Brooks, Crimson Publishing, Nick
	Channer, except for the pictures of Sissinghurst (page 55),
	Penshurst Place (page 58), which are by Jane Rolph
Editorial:	Ark Creative (UK) Ltd
Design:	Ark Creative (UK) Ltd

This product includes mapping data licensed from Ordnance Survey® with the permission of the Controller of Her Majesty's Stationery Office. © Crown Copyright 2014. All rights reserved. Licence number 150002047. Ordnance Survey, the OS symbol and Pathfinder are registered trademarks and Explorer, Landranger and Outdoor Leisure are trademarks of the Ordnance Survey, the national mapping agency of Great Britain.

ISBN: 978-1-85458-533-2

While every care has been taken to ensure the accuracy of the route directions, the publishers cannot accept responsibility for errors or omissions, or for changes in details given. The countryside is not static: hedges and fences can be removed, stiles can become gates, field boundaries can alter, footpaths can be rerouted and changes in ownership can result in the closure or diversion of some concessionary paths. Also, paths that are easy and pleasant for walking in fine conditions may become slippery, muddy and difficult in wet weather, while stepping stones across rivers and streams may become impassable.

If you find an inaccuracy in either the text or maps, please write to Crimson Publishing at the address below.

First published 1993 by Jarrold Publishing Ltd.
Revised and reprinted 1996, 2000, 2003, 2005, 2007.

Printed in Singapore. 7/14

This edition first published in Great Britain 2014 by Crimson Publishing,
The Tramshed, Walcot Street, Bath, BA1 5BB

www.crimsonpublishing.co.uk

A catalogue record for this book is available from the British Library.

Front cover: Thomas a Becket Church at Fairfield, Romney Marsh
Page 1: The Saxon Shore Way at Sandwich

Unearth *The best of* **Britain series**
from Crimson Publishing

Accessible, contemporary guides by local experts

The best of Britain series includes...

Norfolk and Suffolk

The Lake District

Isle of Wight and the New Forest

Northern Ireland

Devon

Cotswolds

Edinburgh and East Coast Scotland

Cornwall and the Isles of Scilly

Peak District

Easy to navigate...informative and packed with practical information - *Which? Holiday*

crimson   www.crimsonpublishing.co.uk